Mothers & Daughters

ALSO BY *Carol Saline* AND *Sharon J. Wohlmuth*

SISTERS

Mothers & Daughters

by

Carol Saline and Sharon J. Wohlmuth

DOUBLEDAY

New York   London   Toronto   Sydney   Auckland

PUBLISHED BY DOUBLEDAY

a division of Bantam Doubleday Dell Publishing Group, Inc.

1540 Broadway, New York, New York 10036

DOUBLEDAY and the portrayal of an anchor with a dolphin
are trademarks of Doubleday, a division of
Bantam Doubleday Dell Publishing Group, Inc.

Book design by Marysarah Quinn

Library of Congress Cataloging-in-Publication Data

Saline, Carol.

Mothers and daughters / essays by Carol Saline ; photographs by Sharon J. Wohlmuth.

p.   cm.

1. Mothers and daughters.   2. Mothers and daughters—Pictorial works.   I. Wohlmuth, Sharon.   II. Title.

HQ755.85.S25   1997

306.874′3—dc21   96-39529

CIP

ISBN 0-385-48125-X

1   3   5   7   9   10   8   6   4   2

First Edition

To my mother, Rebecca, my grandmother Rose, my great-grandmother Ida,
and all of the generations of women who are my mothers.
You are all in my heart.
—S.J.W.

For my mother, Gertrude Auerbach, and my daughter, Sharon Saline.
Because of you, my life is richer, deeper and sweeter.
—C.S.

Acknowledgments

First and foremost we would like to thank our sisters, Beth Josolowitz and Patsy Brandt, who inspired us to create our first book, *Sisters*. Without them, our subsequent collaborations would not have happened. We are most grateful to the many hundreds of women who have contacted us by mail and by phone to share their stories. Your warm response to our work has been our second inspiration. Special thanks to our agent, Ellen Levine, for her friendship, enthusiastic support and guidance; to our editor, Pat Mulcahy, and her assistant, Denell Downum; to Doubleday publisher Arlene Friedman; to our publicists, Judy Hilsinger and Sandi Mendelson; to Bob Asman for his invaluable assistance and infinite patience.

From Carol Saline, a personal thank-you to Eliot Kaplan, editor of *Philadelphia* magazine for buoying me with his confidence in my writing and giving me the time I needed to finish this book; to Ros, Elaine, Joyce, Freyda, Hope and Barbara S. for their loving friendship and invaluable support; and to my dear son, Matthew, who has shown me that sons can be caring and sensitive, too.

From Sharon J. Wohlmuth, a heartfelt thank-you to Betty and her staff; to G. Haynes and G. Foreman, two gifted editors who understood a daughter's need to be with her mother; to S. Wolfe for his knowledge and enlightenment; to J. Sills, the quintessential puzzle solver; to L. Herskowitz, a loving friend; to family and friends who always listen; and to Larry, who loves my mother's hot dog and bean casserole—I promise that I will make more.

Contents

Introductions
xi

Alyce Michaud, her daughter, Pepper Michaud Herman,
her daughter Valerie Herman Rodriguez, and
her daughter, Marly Alyce Rodriguez
3

Carol Murphy and her daughter, Alixandra Matalavage
7

Anne Guisewite and her daughter, Cathy Guisewite
11

Regina Tepfer and her mother, Rose Farro
14

Barbara Jo Saler and her daughters, Amy, Susan,
Alexandra and Stephanie Saler
17

Rosemary Kelly and her daughter, Shawn Kelly
21

Jennifer Moluf and her daughter, Cindy Crawford
23

Louise Nalli and her daughter, Jacqueline Nalli
27

Jeanette LoPiccolo and her daughter, Maria Busciacco, and
her daughter, Deanna Busciacco
30

Janet Leigh and her daughter, Jamie Lee Curtis
33

Adah Askew and her daughter, Jill Bargonetti
37

Ada Balmaseda and her daughters, Elaine Alatriste
and Liz Balmaseda
41

Janet Hauerken and her daughter, Michelle Fryman
44

Ruth Bader Ginsburg and her daughter, Jane Ginsburg
48

Greta White Calfe and her daughter, Verle Morning Star Sayler
52

Brenda Villa and her daughters, Christina and Amanda
55

Yasminka Rukavina and her daughter, Tatjana Rukavina
59

Margaret Atwood and her daughter, Margaret Atwood
62

Laureda Byers and her stepdaughter, Alison Byers
67

Eleanor Cogshall and her daughter, Susan Erb
70

Eleanor Blair and her daughter, Bonnie Blair
73

*Petra Liljestrand and Alice Philipson
and their daughter, Maya*
76

*Darlene Davenport and her daughter,
Susan Davenport*
79

*Nora Cashion and her daughters, Madeline
and Bridget McMahon*
81

Lila Bishop and her daughter, Tara Bishop
85

Edna Austin and her daughter, Patti Austin
87

*Marjorie Margolies Mezvinsky and her daughters,
Holly Mezvinsky and Lee Heh Margolies*
91

Anna Davis and her daughter, Diana Garrett
94

*Lynn Redgrave and her daughters, Kelly and
Annabel Redgrave Clark*
97

Irene Rawlings and her daughter, Liz Rawlings
101

Elsa Malmud and her daughters, Anne and Susan Malmud
105

*Dolly Earl and Barbara Nelson and their daughter,
Lea Jayne Ferrer*
108

Lindy Boggs and her daughter, Cokie Roberts
111

*Ann Clark, her daughter, Catherine Clark Schwartz, and
granddaughters, Rebecca and Hannah*
115

Gwen Sherman and her daughter, Amber Sherman
117

*Sharon Cantrell and her daughters, Christi Driver, Lori
Sommerfeld and Betsy McLaughlin*
121

*Kate Shupe and her daughters, Joan, Nettie, Helen, Mary Lee,
Lula Kate, Jane, Sally, Edith and Maria*
124

Introductions

*I*n the sweet drift before sleep when the mind aimlessly sifts through memories, I picture myself in a vast empty space with my arms outstretched on either side. My right hand reaches toward my mother, a slender, glamorous woman standing erect in high heels. I don't think she owns a pair of flat shoes. Despite her eight decades she's still got a great pair of legs, but her arms betray her age where her tired skin, thin as parchment and easily bruised, hangs like a wrinkled sheet. Her brown hair has turned gray, but that's her secret. She's been coloring it blond as long as I can remember, although I don't think she still believes that blondes have more fun. In fact, the idea of fun seems to have disappeared from her realm of possibility, replaced by an ever-present anxiety over the debilitating aches and pains that dominate her life. Never having had a career of her own, she has never really understood the burdens of mine and chides me constantly about its excessive demands. Worry was always her modus operandi. In her pale blue eyes that once sparkled so gaily, I now see sadness and fear. And it hurts to realize that my mother needs me more than I want her to.

My left hand reaches toward my daughter, a slender woman standing in flat shoes. I think she owns one pair of medium heels. She has my build, my dark hair, my brown eyes. When I was younger people often mistook us for sisters. I loved it; I think she didn't. She is smart and beautiful and a better mother to my grandson than I can remember being to her. She lives 3,000 miles away, which forces us to catalogue shop over the telephone. It's harder to giggle over an awful dress long-distance, but we try. Her childhood brought more joy to my life than I could have imagined. Our struggles in her late adolescence caused me—and no doubt her as well—more pain than my heart could bear. Today she is an adult, terribly busy building her life as a wife, a mother and a psychologist. It hurts to realize my daughter *doesn't* need me nearly as much as I want her to.

My relationship with my eighty-something mother feels like a completed book filled with chapters I'd like to go back and edit—but it's too late. My relationship with my thirty-something daughter feels like a work in progress, one that we will eventually fashion into a masterpiece. And so I stand in the middle, each of them a part of me. I am daughter to mother and mother to daughter, exploding with love for the two most important women in my life.

Why another book on mothers and daughters? Certainly the subject has been amply covered from every possible perspective. After the surprising and wonderful success of *Sisters,* Sharon and I wrestled with what to do next. People said: Surely, you'll do a book on brothers. Or maybe mothers and sons? But ultimately those combinations didn't feel right, and we decided it was best to stay within our own experience. We'd known what it meant to be a sister because we'd lived that relationship. We felt equally at home with mothers and daughters because whatever else a woman may be, each and every one of us is a daughter.

Exactly what it means to be a daughter or a mother is intensely personal. We universally understand that certain words define a mother's role: protect, nurture, love, worry, teach, guide. And there are words that represent a daughter's concerns: caretaking, separation, approval. And while mother can be either a verb or a noun, daughter can be only the latter. There are a million ways "to mother" but "to daughter" has no definition.

This is a relationship built upon the most complex chemistry. It mirrors the bond between sisters in that the ties are fierce and forever. You may or may not have a good relationship with your mother, but you cannot avoid having any kind of relationship at all, in part because you are eternally bound by the steel cords of shared memories. Even death cannot remove a mother's influence from your life. And like sisters, no one can love you more than your mother or hurt you more than your mother.

But in a way significantly different from sisters, mothers and daughters are endlessly changing and reworking their connection.

By the time sisters reach their twenties, their path together is pretty much etched in stone. If they have worked through their sibling rivalries, they most certainly will move forward into a steadily deepening friendship. If they have not yet resolved their conflicts, they will most likely wrangle with their issues the rest of their lives. By contrast, mothers and daughters are companions on an uncharted voyage of discovery along a snaking road often marred by potholes. Crossroads suddenly appear, often lacking clear directions.

Generally speaking, the early years are the easy ones. The mother gives, the daughter takes, and in that fulfillment of mutual needs, they weave the cloth of their future. Here begins the lifelong comfort with each other's bodies, this physical closeness that links a mother to a daughter in a way she can never relate to a son. In so many of our interviews, it was the physical gestures that told the story. The hugs, the kisses, the careless, unconscious touching as natural in adulthood as it was in infancy. As the mother talks, she strokes her daughter's hair. As the daughter talks, she rubs her mother's back, smooths her blouse. Loving mothers and daughters simply could not keep their hands off one another.

By the teen years, the seeds of estrangement have usually begun to sprout. The daughter starts to see herself as separate and different from her mom. The mother struggles with how to hold on to her beloved little girl and, at the same time, give flight to this emerging woman with her own ideas and opinions. Some navigate this tricky passage well; others don't. For them the old conflicts will get painfully replayed in new situations, like a tape stuck in an endless loop.

When and if the daughter becomes a mother herself, a remarkable awakening may occur. In her own mothering, she begins to revisit the life of the woman who bore her. As a new mother, she will clean her baby's drool, change diapers and create a small world of safety. Later as a grown daughter she will repeat these mundane chores in another context, sponging her mother's frail body, feeding and protecting the woman who once did the same for her.

The daughter who mothers discovers the burden of having one channel of her brain constantly on radar alert for her child's well-being. As she cares for her baby, she remembers and appreciates what was given to her by her mother when she was too small to notice. And to her astonishment, she frequently finds herself acting like that woman she swore she'd never be. With humor—or with horror—we daughters inevitably hear the words of our mothers coming from our lips. Put on a sweater. Take your hair out of your eyes. Eat a little something; I made your favorite dish. Don't forget to call. Send a card to Aunt Ida; it's her birthday.

How did this transformation happen? How could you become your mother? Well, being a woman, how could you not?

In the course of interviewing so many women for this book, I began to truly understand that there is no such thing as a normal or typical mother/daughter relationship, in spite of all the myths. That is hardly surprising. This relationship revolves around the struggle of opposites as we waltz together in anger and love. We want so much from each other, yet we would gladly settle for the simple exchange of acceptance. We blame our mothers on one hand and praise them on the other. We shrivel in their disappointment and swell in their pride. We want desperately to be independent while we yearn passionately to be connected.

More than anything in the world, we want our mothers to love us as we want to be loved and our daughters to love us—because we are their mothers. Some might say this is an impossible task. I am convinced that none would argue against the rewards of its pursuit.

Our mothers are our first teachers and the wisest of us become our daughters' students. One of the unexpected bonuses of mothering for me was finding how much I could learn from my daughter and grow from her wisdom. That became a common theme throughout our interviews: Where there is mutual respect,

there is friendship. Where the playing field is competitive and uneven, there is misery.

If I saw one golden thread sewn into every good relationship it was simply expressed in the words "unconditional love." Over and over again, I watched daughters fill up with tears and declare in their own particular way, "I always knew my mother loved me unconditionally and nothing I could ever do would change it." That sense of ongoing support and acceptance said it all. And its absence was the most consistent feature in the presence of difficulty.

Writing *Mothers and Daughters* was an overwhelming emotional experience. In the course of traveling around the country to create this quilt of mother/daughter love, I laughed and cried with the most remarkable women. Sharon and I thank all of them for the precious gift of entering their homes as strangers and leaving as friends because of their willingness to share their deep and intimate feelings. The umbilical cord that connects mothers and daughters can never really be severed. To witness the joy, the delight, the comfort, the sweetness in this love was as close to heaven as I can conjure.

My mother. My daughter. Myself. I stand in the empty space of my dream and gently pull both of them into the circle of my arms. My teachers. My critics. My support system. My friends. My mother. My daughter. Without them, I could not be me.

Carol Saline
1996

❧

My mother left me one morning.
It was November 1991. I was sitting cross-legged, nestled against her on her hospital bed. We were alone. She looked at me, and then she was gone. It was as if she had decided to leave without telling me. I grabbed her shoulders, drew her toward me and confronted her. My voice shook in desperation and anger.

"Mommy, did you just die? You DIED?"—asking her over and over.

I always thought time was endless. I always thought there would be more time to be a daughter. Yet even at the end of her life, in the last eight years when I was her caretaker, I watched our roles shift as I became the mother to her. At the moment she died, she was my mother once again.

I keep my mother alive in my heart by looking at the picture I have of her on my kitchen shelf. There she stands in her kitchen, her cotton apron on—black and white in the photograph, but I know it's the faded blue-and-white-checked one, the one I'd bunch against my face when she left the house so I could inhale her smell. In the picture I know the apron smells rich with her warmth and the triumphs of what she's been cooking. There she is, in her proper sphere, in her strength.

My mother gave me roots and wings. She was the woman who loved to watch me, as a child, climb the large pine trees outside our kitchen window. I knew those branches very well. Some were so fragile they would bend and break, but the danger was thrilling. My mother watched, protecting without restricting, never expressing her fears. It seemed like we were climbing together. Years later, she would remind me, "You climbed the highest." Years later, I would have the realization that in her love she allowed me my own journey.

All of those images are my mother. For me, photographs take their power from memory and emotion. A picture tells its own story, shaped by the mood or insights of the person you are at the time you see it. It becomes layered with the past and the present. It need not be of people you know: if a photograph is powerful, you enter the moment it was taken. All that emerges from your observation becomes your own.

Creating *Mothers and Daughters* was a personal journey, filled with exhilarating highs and excruciating sadness. All the women in our book courageously opened their hearts, and with great trust shared their most intimate feelings with us. Through fragile and fleeting moments, of anger and of laughter, this most profound relationship unfolded before my eyes and heart. Moments that I, like you, have known so well. Moments that reach deep into our souls to define the mother-daughter bond.

I surround myself with the pictures of the women in my life. In a blue frame is Beth, my younger sister, who stands apart from our mother in front of our family home. It is a complex image, one that mirrors their own loving, yet charged, relationship. Close by on the shelf is a picture of my great-grandmother, Ida, who looks out forthrightly—at me, I always feel. Her young daughters left her in Russia to come to America. She encouraged their journey in every sense of the word. She joins the community of women whose line comes down to me.

Because I have no children of my own, I worry that I am the end of that line. But there on the shelf is Rachael. She is not my daughter, she is my husband's child. But at times, because of the love we share, she becomes a daughter to me. Her image joins the others in my heart. This past May, when she rang our bell and I opened the door, she pushed a bouquet of flowers into my hand. I can't even remember what kind they were because I was too overwhelmed by this picture—Rachael, with her blond hair and her lovely smile, and those powerful words: "Happy Mother's Day."

Sharon J. Wohlmuth
1996

Mothers & Daughters

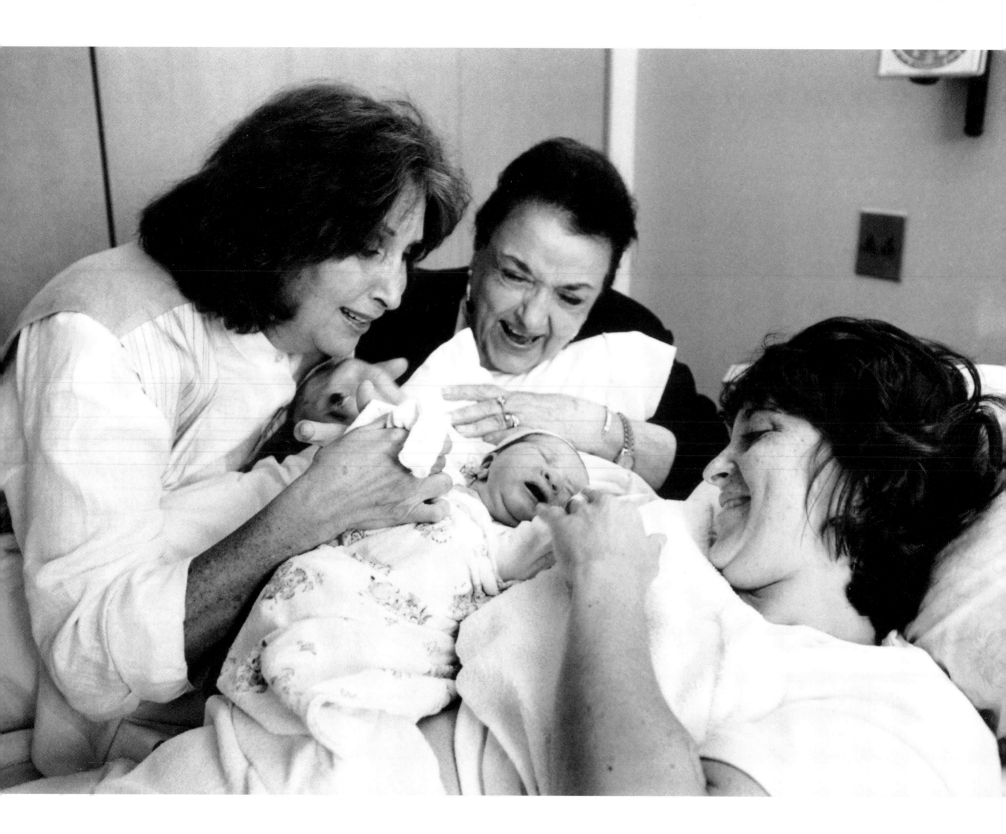

Alyce Michaud, her daughter,
Pepper Michaud Herman,
her daughter, Valerie Herman
Rodriguez, and her daughter,
Marly Alyce Rodriguez

A baby girl is about to be born. Her mother, Valerie, deep in labor, grunts and moans, struggling to bring into the world a tiny replica of herself. All too soon the daughter will become the mother, shaping her own mother/daughter relationship, in her own style, from the clay of her mother's love.

Little one, daughter of Valerie, granddaughter of Pepper, great-granddaughter of Alyce, you will be smothered with the kisses of these powerful women and you will have three tough acts to follow. Your great-great-grandmother came to America in 1923, a refugee widow from Armenia with four children she was determined to educate. A month after arriving, her daughter, Alyce, your great-grandmother, was enrolled at the university. She graduated with a bachelor of science degree and, instead of becoming the doctor her mother had hoped for, she studied singing and acting. Her daughter—your grandmother, Pepper—who was performing in the living room at age two grew up to have the career of her mother's fantasies, first as an actress and later as the voice in countless radio commercials. Pepper returned to college when she was fifty to get the education she'd postponed. She and your mother, Valerie, actually did some commercials together and created a successful board game called Auditions. Your mom is quite a singer in her own right, although she works mainly as a film and video producer. These are your foremothers: three quite different, quite accomplished women united by a common fulfilled desire—they all desperately wanted a special daughter.

Sixty-two years before you were born, your great-grandmother, Alyce, got pregnant on her honeymoon and immediately began praying for a girl because she'd been so close to *her* mother. "I could see the difference between the way my mother talked to my brothers and me," Alyce recalls. "She always addressed me as 'my little girl. I'm going to have the best for my little girl.' It impressed me so much that my mother, an old country woman from Armenia, would be so thrilled to have a daughter. She and I, we were heart to heart. So I said to myself, I must have a girl, too, who will grow up and be a companion to me. Every stage of her life will remind me of a stage I went through. And when the same things happen to her that happened to me, I'll understand.

"So I had my girl, my daughter, Pepper, whom I love so much. It was like having a live doll I could dress in pretty clothes. I felt like a mommy with a play baby. I can still remember, when they put her between my legs in the delivery room, the feel of her wiggling."

Pepper reacted to *her* pregnancy exactly like her mother. She'd also experienced that great close mother/daughter relationship and wanted to repeat the experience with a daughter of her own. She spent the entire nine months before Valerie's birth repeating the mantra: "It's a girl; it's a girl; it's a girl; it's girl."

And then it was Valerie's turn. Her first child was a boy. The second time she became pregnant, Alyce immediately began conditioning her. "Please, darling, you've got to give me a granddaughter. I'm not going to be around much longer. You must have the blessing of a mother-and-daughter relationship. There is nothing like it. I want you to know what it means to have a girl who will grow up and not be just your daughter, but also your friend."

Pepper was every bit as fixated as her mother. When Valerie was four months into her pregnancy, Pepper insisted on accompanying her to the hospital for the amniocentesis test to find out whether she was carrying the next of their long female line. When the report gave an affirmative answer, she was ecstatic and kept asking the doctor, "Are you sure? Are you absolutely sure it's a girl? I can't believe it. This is our dream."

Now Valerie awaits the arrival of that dream with her own vision of how she will mother her daughter. "I'm looking forward to passing on the power and strength that my mother and her mother passed down to me," she says. "I know my daughter will be even stronger than I am, because I will raise her to be independent, to stand up for herself, to say, 'This is what I want and this is what I have to do to get it.'

"I want to teach her what my mother taught me—how to have intimate friendships and how to connect with other women. I am so excited to share with her the female side of myself. Just imagine the joy of having a little version of me walking around. We will sing and dance and laugh—we must have lots of laughter. We'll go shopping for jewelry and I'll buy her little smocked dresses with pink leggings.

"What I most want is for us to have the same kind of girlfriend/mommy relationship I had with my mother: sometimes explosive, but emotional, intimate and loving."

August 6, 1996. 8 P.M. Valerie has been in labor for several hours. Over a Scrabble board in the hospital waiting room, Alyce and Pepper concentrate on their game to keep themselves from thinking about Valerie's pain. Right before Val had checked in, she'd been struck with a sharp contraction and she'd clung to Pepper, crying, "Hold me, Mommy. Hold me." Pepper caressed her with soft words of love and encouragement until the moment passed.

As soon as Valerie was gone, tiny Alyce, eighty-nine years old and thin as a bird, whispered to Pepper, "If I hug you now, will you fall apart?" And on tippy-toes, she reached up to comfort her sixty-two-year-old daughter. "My little Peppy. Don't worry, Valerie will be fine."

To distract each other, they chatter about the baby on her way. "I only wish for Valerie that her little girl will be for her like she was for me," Pepper says.

"If she's got that, she's got it all. I used to call Val my night-light because when everything was dark and gloomy, her brightness and cheer lit up the room. She was perfect. We talked about everything. Nothing was sacred. I remember one long conversation we had the first time she was thinking about going to bed with a boy. The next day I was cooking at the stove and she wrapped her arms around me. 'What's this all about?' I asked. 'I'm so lucky I can talk to you about everything,' she answered. I made a little joke and we laughed and then I sobbed from happiness that she felt so good about our relationship. That's what I want for her and her daughter, heart to heart like my mother taught me, like you can't have with a son."

That story sparks a memory in Alyce. "Pepper, I always told you, let me know when you are not a virgin. One day I was ironing and you were shuffling down the hallway walking funny. I said, 'Did you do something last night you're sorry for today?' And you said you did something, but you weren't sorry for it. That was Harris, and you married him. Do you remember how much we shared? The girl talk. The horse races. Oh my, we fought and we laughed and we loved. I never understood people who said you can't have a best friendship with your daughter."

9:16. The phone rings; they both jump. "Come down to delivery," the nurse says, "and meet Valerie's daughter."

Pepper and Alyce are laughing and crying and hugging each other as they rush to the side of the bed, where a very tired Valerie rocks her moments-old daughter in her arms. Pepper's hands flutter from her daughter to her granddaughter. She is so excited she doesn't know which one of them to touch first. "Oh, Val. Oh, it's little Marly Alyce. Isn't this really what life is all about? I already know this little girl will be my second best friend. This kid is going to be part of me."

"She's so beautiful," Alyce exclaims. "And all that hair! Your mother was completely bald. Is your milk in yet? It's so long ago, I forget when it comes." And with her ancient fingers, she points to each of them and counts aloud. "One, two, three, four. Four generations of mothers and daughters."

It's Marly Alyce's turn now. Time to begin her story. Time to repeat the rich and complex saga shared only by females since time began. Now and forever, every woman born is blessed to be a daughter.

Carol Murphy and her daughter, Alixandra Matalavage

*I*n the weathered barn that serves as the country store at Murphy's Farm, this little hand-lettered sign sits on an antique player piano:

In July of 1992 we suffered heavy rains and high temperatures which caused our sweet cherries to crack and split, destroying virtually our entire crop. My daughter Xandy, who was here visiting for two weeks from Okinawa, in a desperate effort to salvage something from our crop, began making jams and jellies and canning cherries. She didn't leave the kitchen for three days when she had to abandon the effort to get some sleep. The beautiful array of jams, jellies and relishes you see on our shelves today is what has grown from that desperate three-day endeavor. Xandy has now joined me in the business and is completely responsible for all our food processing. As you can see, she rarely leaves the kitchen, but if you should run into her, please tell her that I love her.

Carol Murphy

When Carol Murphy marched out of the University of Pennsylvania twenty-some years ago with a degree in biochemistry, it's highly unlikely that even the most gifted psychic could have convinced her that she'd end up divorced, owning a fruit farm and running it with her daughter. That simply was not what she believed life had destined for her.

She and her husband, an engineer, really had no intention of working the farm when they bought it as a tax shelter in the early 1980s. Eight months later, the house, which was far more valuable than the sixty-five acres of land on which it sat, caught fire. Not long after, the marriage was also in ashes.

"There I was, thirty-five years old with three young children, two sons and a daughter," Carol remembers. "It wasn't a question of staying on the farm or leaving it, because I was left with a $100,000 mortgage, now worth $20,000 because the house was ruined." So she moved the kids into a trailer on the grounds and learned to harvest the farm's fruit trees to pay their bills. "Farming's not that complicated," she explains. "Crops don't give you a whole lot of choice, because when they're ready to pick, you pick them. Nature shoves you into making decisions."

Carol has a practical way of looking at things, even when life is whacking her hard. Like the time of the custody battle, which ended with her temporarily losing her daughter, Alixandra (whom she calls Xandy). There was plenty of pain on Carol's end, but Xandy suffered the real damage. "The divorce just squashed something," her mother says. From a straight-A student, president of the student council, she became a miserably unhappy teenager.

It didn't help the distressed adolescent that her father kept telling her how much she resembled her mother, someone for whom he obviously had little respect.

"It was at a time when I was becoming a woman," Xandy remembers, "and I felt it was wrong to be like my mother because that made my father unhappy, which I didn't want to do. But I didn't want to hurt my mother and make her unhappy either. So I ended up feeling terrible about myself.

"Years later I realized what a compliment my father was giving me. My mother is so determined. When she sets her mind to something, boom, it gets done. How great for me to be like her."

In the meantime, however, Xandy had to find out who she was. In her sophomore year of college, after spending more time hitting the bottle than hitting the books, she quit and joined the Marines.

"I needed to give myself a kick in the behind," Xandy says, "and it worked. Until then I was a rebellious little snot." Her mother learned of her enlistment when a "Dear Mrs. Murphy" letter from the Marine Corps arrived in the mail. "It never occurred to me she might be angry," Xandy says. "I had done the most horrible things in the world you could imagine, but she was always there for me. I have always been very secure in my mother's love."

It's hard to pinpoint exactly whose idea it was for Xandy to come home to help with the farm. In Xandy's version, she called her mother from Japan. "Probably collect," she says. "Mom asked me if I'd thought about what I was going to do when I got out of the military. She said she was losing her enthusiasm for farming and could use some help. That was just the best compliment in the world. That my mother would want me to be a part of what she'd done, of something she'd put so much into. My mom is my hero. My role model. There's so much about her I aspire to."

At that point, after fifteen years of struggling to make a go of her orchards, Carol Murphy "was ready to throw in the towel. I was burned out. It seemed like I was surviving, but I wasn't progressing. I had ideas, but no energy to implement them."

Xandy brought enough can-do enthusiasm for both of them, and if either had the slightest doubt about how they could work together, it was resolved by the applesauce.

Carol was attending a planning meeting for the local Apple Festival when a man from the Chamber of Commerce mentioned they'd like to have a signature product from the growers of their county to promote the region. He turned to her. "You're a farmer. You have fruit orchards. Do you make applesauce?"

"Oh, we make wonderful applesauce," Carol answered. Then she ran home and called Xandy, who by then had returned to the States and was stationed in Virginia. "How the hell do you make applesauce?" she asked.

Xandy, who'd always been interested in cooking and kept a stash of her grandmother's recipes, gave Carol the instructions over the phone and the result was so delicious that the Chamber ordered 300 jars. That weekend, and every one thereafter for nearly a year, Xandy drove several hundred miles to the farm from Quantico Marine Base and made applesauce—and jellies—and jams—and relishes, all from the variety of fruits Carol produced on the farm. Immediately upon her discharge, Xandy moved in with her two toddlers (and later her husband).

The five of them now live in cramped quarters in the shell of the burned-out farmhouse that Carol has been slowly restoring for over a decade. Xandy whips up her preserves in a large sun-drenched kitchen, paneled with planks from trees Carol cut down herself. It opens into a warm, cozy living room lined with bookshelves; a stereo in the corner is usually playing classical music. Antique rugs spill over the weathered original floorboards. The rest of the house remains a work in progress and only recently has Carol been able to move into an apartment of sorts on the second floor, relinquishing her bedroom and the one bath to Xandy's family.

"I am very fastidious," Carol points out, "and Xandy lives in utter chaos, but that's okay. In business, where it counts, we have no conflicts whatsoever." Carol handles the outside—grows the fruit, worries about the sprays, organizes the store in the barn. Xandy creates the products and—in the long, dark nights of a Buffalo, New York, winter—she develops small handicrafts to sell in the store.

They actually worry about too much contented togetherness. "We don't really need anybody else," Carol says. "We are our own social contact, own best friends, own business associates. The biggest danger in our relationship is cutting ourselves off from other people."

Clearly, Carol has been rejuvenated by Xandy's presence. "She is totally on my side. My biggest supporter. To have your daughter as your partner makes all the difference." Despite the thrill of building a business together, Carol would have preferred that Xandy returned to a thriving enterprise, flowering with profit. "It bothers me," she says, "that Xandy knows me as somebody who struggled and didn't get very far."

"That's funny," Xandy says. "I guess you can't see the orchard for the trees. When I see the barn needs painting, I don't view that as a failing of my mother's. I look at it as 'just wait till we can get this done.' I think her ideas are wonderful."

"Wonderful," Carol teases her, "is having somebody you can talk to about the business who tells you the brochures you made stink."

Thus far, money issues haven't cropped up because there isn't much left after the bills are paid. But that's changing. "We used to buy canning jars for our preserves as we needed them," Carol says. "This year, we thought we reached the big league and ordered 60 cases of pint jars and 70 cases of half-pints. In a few months we bought 200 more cases of pints and a hundred more of half-pints. We cleaned them out and put in an order for another 500 cases. We've added pumpkins and hayrides and school trips. Our expansion is overwhelming."

If they did ever have a serious difference of opinion, Xandy insists she would always defer to her mother—but you can bet there'd be lots of discussion first. These two women like to talk, especially to each other. And to dream. Of a day when they'll turn the refurbished farmhouse into a bed-and-breakfast. Of a time when there will be money in the bank at the end of the year.

"I expect in ten years we'll be like we are now, except I'll be a bit grayer," Carol says. "We'll still be believing in each other, believing in what we're doing and building on what we have."

"This farm is really the only place I want to be," Xandy says. "I love it here. Being outside. The change of seasons. I love this house and I love that my kids and I are with my mom. Sometimes we get so crazy busy I forget that she'd be my friend even if she wasn't my mom. The other night I just stopped and gave her a hug and said I'm sorry that I don't remember more often to tell you how much I appreciate the fact that you're my mother."

And how proud she is to be the farmer's daughter!

Anne Guisewite and her daughter, Cathy Guisewite

Cathy, the cartoon character, is standing in a department store having a conversation with her mother.

"What do you want for Christmas, Mom?" she asks.

"Well, I'd like you to get back together with the young men you alienated over Thanksgiving and for one of them to give you a great big diamond ring in a velvet box. Then you'll get married, have a baby, start wearing pretty hats like Princess Diana and live happily ever after in a beautiful castle."

A salesgirl approaches them. "Can I help you?" Cathy looks dejectedly at her mom and says, "I don't think so."

Does art imitate life? Is Cathy Guisewite's real mother, Anne, the noodge she's portrayed as in the strip?

"Actually, my mother is infinitely more discreet about bringing up husbands and grandchildren," Cathy admits. "I'm usually exaggerating or projecting what I think she thinks."

On the other hand, Anne Guisewite did start buying silver for Cathy's wedding when she was just a baby. "For one birthday, she'd give me a silver fork. The next year, maybe a spoon. It was very sweet," Cathy explains. "I don't know anybody else's mother who actively collected their wedding silver from the time they were an infant. When I got to be thirty-five she had the whole set and it was clear I was not vaguely close to any relationship that was leading to marriage, so she gave it to me. It was one of those very touching moments. Sad because Mom was saying I'm giving up this dream, yet acknowledging that I had the life I wanted and I didn't need to be married to use real silver forks."

And the mother, who really does speak in clichés, answers: "Well, you've done great. You were a beautiful daughter to raise and you're a successful career lady. What do I have to be upset about? Of course, you could still find Mr. Wonderful and live happily ever after."

They both giggle. "I think the truest thing in the comic strip is Cathy's relationship with her mom," says the soft-spoken writer. "It's a rich tangle of genuine devotion, anxiety, frustration, friendship, love, a need for dependence and a need for independence. Lots of butting heads. Around Mom, I still behave like a six-year-old. Stubborn. Obstinate. Belligerent. Taking offense where none was intended. Being contrary for the joy of being contrary."

"It's your typical, generic mother/daughter relationship," Anne sums up. "No matter how old your child is, you still think of her as a child."

Poor Cathy Guisewite, burdened by having this June Cleaver role-model mother who hung every picture she drew on the refrigerator, told her repeatedly how wonderful she was and spooned approval on her like sugar on cereal.

Like her cartoon self, Anne often feels like a set of encyclopedias that no one opens. But that doesn't stop her from bombarding her three daughters with useful information, always appropriately packaged and addressed.

Cathy's sister Mickey—who is ten years younger, writes a syndicated humor column and has a toddler—gets the early-childhood material.

Mary Anne—two years older, an artist and homemaker with teenagers—gets the envelopes filled with insights on adolescent sexuality.

Cathy, the workaholic middle child, winds up with a smattering of everything.

"The packages always arrive with a note saying something like 'I know you'll hate this because I'm your mother but it will be really GOOD for you.' Cathy explains, "We all have entire libraries of yoga tapes. Not the ones you buy but videos she actually spent hours recording from her TV.

"Instead of baking muffins when we grew up, Mom used to steam vegetables with brown rice. Now she mails us piles of health books, not to mention cases of vitamins and vitamin programs with instruction books. And clippings of all sorts, especially Ann Landers columns. She can't read a newspaper without holding a scissors in her hand. And she only reads as a disbursement thing. She got so cramped clipping *The Wall Street Journal* that she finally sent me a subscription. And she still clips it anyway."

"That's because you don't read it," Anne says, undaunted.

Lucky Cathy Guisewite: Lacking tragedy for inspiration, she finds humor in her practically perfect Mom and makes us laugh at the angst of ordinary problems like messy closets, dateless weekends, fat thighs and doting mothers with flawless advice.

"My mother is such a master in the support area that she almost invites my abuse," Cathy says good-naturedly. "If I'm concerned about something and I tell her, she'll always volunteer a solution."

"And you'll always reject my advice," Anne counters.

"Not only do I reject it, I'm annoyed you gave it—even though I asked," Cathy responds, smiling. "Or maybe I just want something to reject. I guess what's most aggravating is that Mom's solutions, however simplistic, are usually pretty much the right road to follow. I don't like her to be right. And even though I can't stand wanting her approval, it's critical that I get it. And most aggravating is when she does things that make me crazy, like trying to accommodate everybody's feelings, because she's doing what I most hate in myself that makes me exactly like her."

To tell the truth, Anne Guisewite grew up wanting to be Cathy. "I wanted to be a great writer, lead an adventurous life. Then I met Mr. Perfect in college and that took care of it. I became so fascinated with my children—and how their little personalities developed—that I didn't want to miss one minute of their lives." So without any resentment, she simply bequeathed her dream to her daughter.

"Because Mom was a writer at heart she always encouraged us

to express our feelings on paper instead of gossiping about them. I wrote some tragic journals growing up."

After college Cathy landed a great job in an advertising agency. But her personal life was a shambles. "I had a horrible love life. I was overweight. I'd spend every evening eating, writing in my journal and hoping this guy I was obsessed with would call. I got tired of writing the same misery over and over, so I started summing up my feelings in picture form and sending these very personal drawings home to Mom. I guess I was showing her: Look, I got it on paper."

"I felt so badly I couldn't help Cathy," Anne says, "but I could see she was living like thousands of young women, trying to make it in a world hampered by roles they'd been expected to assume growing up. I thought these cartoons were very clever and she was on to something. I told her she should try to publish them. She was horrified and said, 'Of course you think they're special. You're my mom.'"

Having Anne Guisewite for a mother means never having to worry who will bug you. "She was relentless," Cathy recalls. "She went to the library, looked up information on selling comic strips, did all the research, wrote lists of syndicators and the order in which I should submit them. Finally I did it just to get her off my back."

The first syndicate company she approached sent her a contract. They liked the energy in the characters and felt confident she could learn to draw better. For several months, Cathy, who does not consider herself a funny person, secretly set her alarm for 3 A.M. to write the strip before going into work.

Anne, of course, assumed the role of cheerleader. "She's my daughter. I can't stop worrying about her. She was working her tail off in that ad agency and I thought this might be the answer."

Naturally, Anne was completely right. "Cathy" the comic strip is now twenty years old and more popular than ever. And Anne, prodded by her daughter, has published her own book of helpful hints called *Motherly Advice from Cathy's Mom* (with illustrations by you know who).

Cathy will tell you that she doesn't do nearly enough for her mother. Anne, of course, will tell you Cathy is very generous and she's simply grateful to share part of her life, especially now that there's a grandchild in it.

No, Mr. Wonderful did not come along. Cathy finally decided a dog wasn't enough to fulfill her maternal instincts. At forty-one, she paid her mother the ultimate compliment and adopted a daughter.

"I only wanted a girl so I could relive my relationship with my mom—with me being her. She made me feel that motherhood was an experience I did not want to miss. I hope I'm raising Ivy with all the stuff I love about my Mom, although I'll never have her patience. When I watch Mom with Ivy and she knows exactly how to let a three-year-old's imagination develop, I have a newfound respect for her. To be the kind of mother she was and is, you have to totally be there for someone else. I'm way too selfish for that."

"But wait," Anne Guisewite chimes in automatically, "you're providing Ivy the most wonderful, loving care." Suddenly they both burst out laughing. Anne is at it again.

Regina Tepfer and
her mother, Rose Farro

"Hey, Mom, can you hear me? I know you're *there.*"

Regina softly massages her belly over the spot where her dead mother's kidney lies inside her, totally useless.

Twice her mother gave her the priceless gift of life. Once at birth; once at death. But the second gift was rejected.

When a stroke felled seventy-three-year-old Rose Farro in the middle of a gin game, doctors were able to maintain her on life support until arrangements could be made to remove her kidney and implant it into her desperately ill daughter. Regina had been weakening on dialysis for nearly a year while awaiting a transplant. But despite a massive infusion of antirejection drugs, her body refused to accept her mother's death-wish donation.

"This isn't fair, Mom. Sometimes when I'm feeling really sorry for myself, I get angry with you because you died and left me, and then the kidney didn't even work.

"I should have been thrilled to get it. But I didn't want yours. I wanted *you.* Alive. It was so awful coming to the hospital and seeing you hooked up to all those machines. I couldn't get close enough to hold you and hug you. I kept telling you how much I loved you. Did you hear me? I tried to believe you were going to get better, but the doctors said you'd already passed away, and they were keeping you on life support for my sake. I kept thinking that if they didn't disconnect the machines, you'd come around. Of course I was kidding myself.

"Everybody—the family, the doctors—pressured me, saying that this was what *you* wanted. That you were presenting me with a second chance at life. I'll admit I was disappointed when no one else in the family offered, but I never expected it

from you, sick as you were from heart surgery and having had your leg amputated. When I learned that, months before, you'd gone to my doctor and volunteered to give me one of your kidneys, I was so surprised! That broke my heart even more because I couldn't even say thank you.

"In a weird way, I was really happy when the doctors told me, after the rejection, that they'll never have to remove it—even when I get a new kidney. I don't know how much I could go on if they took it out. Even though it's eerie having a part of you in me, it's comforting, too. I like that I can put my hand over your kidney and talk to you. Kind of like you're still here. Except you're not where I really want you—at the other end of the phone line.

"It's so hard not to call you. So hard. You know how it is when you first get sick, *everybody* calls you. But then as it goes along, people have things to do, children to care for, and they just forget. Not you, Mom. God, we talked ten, eleven times a day and you had a way of always making me feel things would get better.

" 'Let's go out to lunch,' you'd say. 'Let's have dinner. Come on over and we'll play cards.' And when it would get dark, you'd tell me, 'It's getting late. You better go home, Regina.' I only lived fifteen minutes away, but you were always worried whether I'd get home okay. . . . Nobody worries about me anymore.

"I reminisce a lot about how close we were when I was growing up. You loved me so much. Anything I wanted to get involved in was fine with you. Piano lessons. Dancing lessons.

Camping. How you hated camping! But you did it for me. I couldn't stand sleeping on the dirty ground. You took Dad's station wagon so my friends and I could sleep in the car. And you slept outside with the counselors. And all those beautiful clothes you made me in high school. You could sew up a storm; I have trouble with buttons.

"To tell you the truth, Mom, I'm not in such good shape. Every time I turn around, something goes wrong, and I'm back in the hospital. My marriage is finished. No big surprise. When I first got sick, the social worker told me that about twenty percent of marriages don't work out because the spouse can't deal with the strain of kidney failure. I was never good at picking husbands anyway.

"I've moved back alone to your old house. Everything I do is an effort, and I seem to spend most of my time on home dialysis. I'm on the list for another kidney. But it could take years.

"Two months ago I was very depressed, but I kicked myself in the butt and said I'm going to get it together. I want Mom to be proud of me. Isn't it funny! No matter how old you are, you still want your mom to be proud of you. I wish I could be more positive like you were. And more forgiving. You were always telling me to forgive people who had hurt me. 'Don't be angry and hold grudges,' you'd say. 'It's not worth it.'

"I'm trying, Mom. But I just can't forgive you. For dying and leaving me alone."

Barbara Jo Saler and her daughters, Amy, Susan, Alexandra and Stephanie Saler

"Sometimes you have to give up your children so you can get them back," says Barbara Saler, stretching her arms to embrace all four of her beautiful daughters. She is so grateful that the scars from their family trip through hell have almost healed.

Amy was twenty, Susan, fifteen, and the twins, Ali and Stephie, just eleven when Barbara's husband announced that their marriage was over. Kaput. Finished. And he was taking the children. Since he'd always ruled the roost and made every decision, his word was law.

"I was devastated," Barbara remembers. "A total basket case. I had never worked. I had no college education. I was paralyzed with fear over how I would survive. And on top of that, I'd just lost my children." Only Amy, the oldest and most mature, elected to stay with her mother.

"Dad told us we were going to live with him and that's the way it was. That's what we wanted," says Ali, sobbing with Stephie and Susan as they relive the awful memory of how they rejected their mother. "We were stupid, spoiled brats. Before our parents divorced, we'd had this charmed life, like a fairy tale. We knew Dad would take care of us, take us shopping. That's what you think about when you're eleven. Yourself. You don't think how your mom will feel."

Especially if you view her as a doormat. "Dad was like a god," Susan explains. "He was everything to us and essentially took the role of motherhood away from Mom. She was a very weak person then, totally different. We didn't respect her. Her parents, her husband, everyone had always railroaded her. Told her what to do, where to be, who to marry, how to raise her kids. She never made any decisions. Never stood up for herself. Mom was in the background, doing drudgery like our homework with us. Always trying to accommodate. She got stuck with all the crap and Dad got all the glory."

When her daughters flat out told her, "We don't want to live with you," Barbara chose not to fight for them. "In my heart I knew that they were young and wanted to be taken care of and feel safe. They thought their father would provide that," she says. "A wonderful psychiatrist kept telling me, 'Barbara, you put so much good stuff into those girls. They won't forget you.' "

Against the advice of her friends, Barbara remained passive. "A custody battle would have cut up the girls in little pieces. There was no way they could be with me *and* with their father. So why make everybody miserable? But I never gave up loving them. And I bit my tongue a million times to keep from saying or doing anything that would make them feel so guilty they couldn't come

back. I sent them birthday cards. I called them occasionally, just to tell them that I loved them, that I understood, and I was there. But it was terribly painful because they didn't want to talk to me. Sometimes people would say, 'God, your daughters don't want to live with you,' as if I'd done something so awful to drive them away."

Stephie once caught a glimpse of her mother while shopping at The Gap and ran out of the store to avoid her. "I was trying to make my world okay, and Mom was a threat to that," she says awkwardly, still grappling with her guilt. Barbara wasn't even welcome at her twins' bat mitzvah, the momentous rite of passage when a Jewish daughter turns thirteen. She thought about sitting in the back of the synagogue. "But I knew it would only make the girls feel embarrassed and nervous and I'd be there crying and they wouldn't come give me a hug."

"Looking back," Ali tries to explain, "she was our mom, but she wasn't. We were separated from her." Ultimately that separation from her children and her husband became Barbara's emancipation proclamation.

"I realized I'd never had a chance to grow up and develop myself," she says. "I looked at my life and saw these were the cards I'd been dealt. I could be depressed, furious and miserable or stop feeling sorry for myself and take this as a wonderful opportunity to become a role model for my daughters and show them what an independent woman can do if she is not afraid of life. For twenty-three years of marriage, I'd been depending on someone else to make my life better. Now I was going to do it on my own."

Turning to her love of flowers, she started a small business delivering weekly arrangements to offices which developed into a successful career as a floral consultant for parties and events. Meanwhile she hoped for the day when her girls would come live with her and occupy the beds she had waiting for them in her apartment. It took nearly three years.

Amy and Ali made the first contact. When Amy had chosen to

stay with her mother, she'd also been cut off from her sisters and she seemed less daunting for Ali to approach. "I asked Amy to set something up with Mom," Ali recalls. "I didn't know how to do it on my own and I couldn't even remember what I was mad about. Our meeting was kind of weird. We were both scared of each other. Mom was shaking and couldn't speak and then she just opened her arms."

Ali's reconciliation led to Stephie's, and then it was Susan's turn. The impetus came from a financial issue with her father that gave her the excuse she needed to reunite with her mother, whom she'd been missing terribly. "I never knew what real, unconditional love was until then, because everything had always had a price tag."

Barbara remembers the anguish in Susan's voice when she asked if she could come to live with her. "She was so afraid how I'd react and I just said: When can I pick you up? That was it."

The mother Susan, Ali and Stephie reunited with bore little resemblance to the mother they'd fled. "It was like night and day," Susan exclaims. "I guess we all grew up," Ali points out. "But Mom grew the most. She's so strong now. So admirable. She's more than our mother. She's our role model and friend. I hate to say it, but when I look back, she didn't have much of a personality. Now she has likes and dislikes. She's not afraid to speak her mind. She's taught me how important it is to be there for other people. But you can't forget to take care of yourself."

Amy says, "As a child I always thought grown-ups knew everything and had stopped learning. Watching my mother develop, getting better and better and more confident in her profession and herself, I realize that life can be an ongoing journey. I used to resist her taste; now I see myself turning into her, and I welcome it."

Stephanie speaks for all her sisters when she tearfully talks about how remarkable it is that despite the hurt they heaped on their mother, she never blamed them and never stopped loving them. "We were all victims to some extent," she says, "and we all came out winners. We are very lucky."

Susan has grown to appreciate her mother's spirituality. "She has taught us about the beauty in small details. I always kid her because she'll walk down the street and stop to examine the petals on a flower or delight in how exquisite a cloud formation is."

It's been four years since Barbara Saler's girls came back, and today the five are so tightly bonded it would be hard to squeeze a hair between them. The girls have moved on to college and jobs in other cities, but home will always be at Mom's.

"She'll pick us up from the train and cook a wonderful dinner, probably pasta, and we won't get up from the table for at least four hours," Ali says. "Then we'll get undressed and climb in her bed and talk some more. In a way, I'm glad this happened to us because we're all better people. I'm scared to think of what I would have become. Stephie and I both work to help put ourselves through school. We've been rich and poor and we've survived. By Mom showing us she could take care of herself emotionally and financially, now we know that we can, too."

They're forever catching up on the years they lost. "The last time I was home, Mom was putting makeup concealer under my eyes," Stephie, now nineteen, says. "And it was so wonderful. She didn't do that when I was thirteen. We missed sharing our adolescence with her."

And they still have so much to learn from each other. "If there is anything I can teach these wonderful human beings who are my daughters," Barbara says, "it's that anger and bitterness are like shackles around you. We have to move forward. My prayer is that any bit of guilt they still harbor, any remnants of remorse, will disappear. It's not going to prove their love for me in any way. It was always there and it always will be. That's why they came back."

Rosemary Kelly and
her daughter, Shawn Kelly

S hawn Kelly was three years old when her father abandoned her. In the ten years since, she's received two cards, one phone call and a hundred dollars in child support, and, if it ends there, that's fine with her. "I've got this great mom," she says cheerily. "None of my friends have moms like her. They're all jealous. She's active; she's fun; she's funny. The best way I can describe her is that she's not a dork."

From Shawn's perspective there are nothing but advantages to being the one-and-only. "My mom gives me all her attention. When we go to the mall, I'll get all these clothes and she'll just buy a scarf.

"When I get in trouble, there's just one person to yell at me.

"We get to have lots of mother/daughter talks. There's nothing I couldn't ask her or tell her.

"And we do lots of girl things, like when she dries my hair or we lie out in the sun and go swimming and to the movies.

"And we cuddle."

Rosemary interrupts, laughing. "Right, like the time your third-grade teacher called to tell me you said your mother abused you. When she asked you what I did, you said, 'She kisses my face all the time.'"

These two dark-haired beauties with their luminous eyes and bright laughter look and act a lot like sisters. Rosemary's real sister has Down's syndrome and lives thousands of miles away with their mother, whom Rosemary calls daily. Perhaps because she and Shawn live so far from their extended family, it has helped them develop an especially sweet and tender compatibility. They often finish each other's sentences and surprise themselves by choosing the same clothes.

Like any mother who has raised a daughter alone, Rosemary often feels overwhelmed by the financial and emotional responsibilities. "Everything is on my shoulders. Whenever it's time to be the bad guy, I'm always it. I wish I could manage to do more for Shawn. For example, I have this great job as a flight attendant and we could fly anywhere for a vacation, but we don't go because we can't afford it. Money is always tight. I remember once Shawn was playing volleyball and the other girls and their families were going out to eat after the game. That particular night I just couldn't afford a pizza, so I had to lie and say we had something else to do. I felt awful."

Other times she feels downright guilty for the demands she places on Shawn. "Because it's just the two of us, I depend on her more than I want to. Sometimes when she's helping me around the house I think: When I was a child I never had to iron and scrub the bathroom and vacuum. I got to do little-girl things and Shawn has to pitch in so much more than I ever did."

Rosemary has saved every card, note or drawing Shawn has given her over the years, and when she's off working for three or four days, she always carries a little packet of "Shawn" mementos. "When I'm in my hotel room all by myself, I read them and think what a neat kid she is. She actually wrote to the Vatican when the Pope was coming to Colorado and invited him to a barbecue at our house. Can you imagine! There are times I get stomachaches from laughing with her. She does this great Elvis imitation. She just knocks me out."

"Well, I guess if I weren't around, Mom wouldn't laugh as much," Shawn says shyly.

Rosemary digs into her collection of Shawn's notes. "Listen to this one. She wrote it to a friend of mine who was having trouble with her husband and came to stay here one night to get her head together: 'I hope you have a good night's sleep. You need it. I left you some towels if you want to take a shower or wash your face. You are a very, very nice lady. This should not be happening to you. Don't worry. Things will get better. Love and friendship, Shawn.' Is there any wonder that I can't wait to get home from a trip to see her face and hear her voice? I really miss her."

"That's why," Shawn says with mock exasperation, "she tells me I can't date until I'm forty. And when I get married, she's not going to give me away, she's going to let someone borrow me."

Rosemary is back rummaging in her mementos. "Look at this one. It's a Father's Day card Shawn sent me one year. I asked her, 'Honey, why did you do that?' She said, 'Well, Mom, you taught me how to swim, taught me how to ride my bike, how to roller-skate. I think a lot of dads would have done that. You're the one who always does everything for me, so I bought you a Father's Day card.'"

Shawn blushes. "Well, since I don't have a dad, Mom is my dad. She's my best friend and in some ways when she is sick, she's like my daughter because I take care of her. She's my sister, too. She taught me to put my family before all else. She's just my everything."

On hearing her daughter's tribute, Rosemary can't control her sobs. It takes several minutes for her to compose herself and answer, "You are my life, Shawn. I would die without you."

Jennifer Moluf and her daughter, Cindy Crawford

When Cindy Crawford decided to appear topless in *Playboy* magazine, the last thing she worried about was her mother's approval. "Obviously part of the way I think about everything is through a filter my mother helped establish," the supermodel says. "By the time I'd reached high school, Mom more or less said, 'I've had all the influence I can have; I'll now respect any choices you make.' She was confident enough in the tools she gave me that she trusted my decisions."

What did concern Cindy was how her mother would be treated by the conservative folks in her middle-American hometown of De Kalb, Illinois, where Jennifer Moluf gets lots of attention as the mom of the only local celebrity.

"If somebody wanted to be jealous or catty, this was the perfect opportunity," Jennifer explains. "Cindy, being who she is, was concerned about my well-being."

"I remember calling Mom to warn her so she'd be armed for however people acted," Cindy remembers. "I said it was okay if she didn't like the photos, but she shouldn't judge them in advance because of the connotation *Playboy* has. Frankly, if the same photos had been in *Vogue,* nobody would have said a thing."

As it turned out, the sight of Cindy Crawford topless didn't create much of a stir in town or with her mother. "When I saw the photos, I was relieved," Jennifer says. "I thought, oh, these are great. No problem! I can handle this."

Handling her famous daughter's star-studded life has never been any problem for Cindy Crawford's mother. Although their lifestyles are vastly different, their lives are grounded in the same traditional values and both of them envision a future for Cindy that includes a station wagon with kids in the backseat.

"I do worry about the industry she's in," Jennifer says, "because there's so much instability and lack of family morals. I know how important these are to me as well as to Cindy. I hope I've had something to do with the fact that she's stayed quite close to me and her sisters [one older, one younger], and we continue to share all the things that are important in our lives."

"I am a product of my upbringing," Cindy says. "We went to church every Sunday and were taught to respect our parents. I've always looked to my mom for support and trusted her advice. There was a time she was afraid to give it because she'd say, 'My life is so different from yours.' But we've both come to realize that our values aren't different at all; we just operate in different arenas. Coming home to Mom's house is like food to fuel the rest of my life."

"That's because I always make sure to have plenty of Swiss Miss for you to drink," Jennifer kids her, offering up a tray of Rice Krispies treats she's baked. "What's so nice about Cindy's visits is that she can come home, and even though we usually speak on the phone three or four times a week, I may not have seen her for months. We just flop on the bed, talk and laugh, throw some tuna on the grill or hang around the pool, like we'd seen each other yesterday."

A house with a swimming pool was certainly far beyond the reach of the Crawfords when Cindy was growing up. Her father worked in construction and her mother, married and pregnant at seventeen, stayed home with the four children. (The youngest, a son, died at age four.) Hordes of Jennifer's relatives lived nearby and they were always getting together. No holiday went uncelebrated, and the favorite entertainment was usually Cindy and her two sisters doing their imitation of the Supremes. Meanwhile her parents were singing a less harmonious melody, and by the time Cindy was in high school they'd split.

"After my dad moved out we had a small house with only one bathroom," Cindy remembers. "There was no way with four women you could have any privacy. One of us would be in the tub, one brushing her teeth, one going to the bathroom. That's where we'd all talk. We never fought, except for the typical stuff over curling irons, clothes and boys. We're all more like best friends."

When a photographer first spotted Cindy in a mall and suggested she think about modeling, the family didn't have the $500 for head shots to create a portfolio. But they began saving. The lure wasn't the glamour; it was the earning potential. Cindy, a straight-A student, originally pursued modeling as a way to raise tuition money to augment her scholarship to Northwestern University. But she became successful so quickly that her academic dreams went up in smoke.

"I always wanted to make a mark," Cindy says. "I knew I'd do something different, but I never expected it to be modeling. That was just a good way to make money. It was never my dream."

"Actually Cindy thought she'd be the first woman president," her mother interjects. "That was in seventh grade when she'd discovered the Equal Rights Amendment and feminism. Women who didn't have careers weren't high on her list."

"That was probably the hardest time I had with my mom," Cindy admits. "She didn't work, which now I think was great, but then I didn't respect her very much. I didn't see where she had any power in our house. She was a real Pollyanna."

"That's when the girls used to call me Polly," Jennifer says.

"But as a grown-up," Cindy goes on, "I realize now what a gift my mom's outlook is. Of all the ways to be, it's sure better to laugh and have joy. Even when our baby brother died, she grieved, but she got through it. I remember she was so cool. My older sister was in fifth grade and didn't want to go to the funeral. I did. Mom gave us the choice of doing what we wanted, and nobody got rewarded or punished for what they chose."

"Losing a child taught me that you can't own anybody's life," Jennifer explains. "You have to let people be themselves and accept them for who they are."

"Mom's the kind of person," Cindy points out, "who will give herself the burned hamburger off the serving plate and give the best to others. We girls never felt that if we did something better or made more money or had a better boyfriend or got a better grade, we would get any more of her love. I think she was just relieved she got three girls through high school without any of us getting pregnant or arrested."

Whoa! Are there any dark secrets in Cindy's past?

"Not really. I did wash her mouth out with soap occasionally. But she was basically a good child. Only when she was bad, she was horrid. At two or three, she'd have these little tantrums if I disciplined her. She'd stomp off into her bedroom, put her head under her pillow, tuck her legs under her body and go to sleep. In two hours she'd wake up in the best mood you ever saw.

"She was always into clothes. In sixth grade she told me not to do her wash anymore because I didn't do it correctly. She'd wash her own jeans and press them a certain way. Everything had to be just so. She had long hair and was very particular about it, too. But she did like to have me braid it and brush it. And I remember being called into the principal's office a few times because she was correcting the English teacher's grammar in class."

"Oh, I was something," Cindy cuts in. "I would rewrite my mom's notes to the school because she does this random capitalization and punctuation thing, and I'd be so embarrassed."

That blip of pettiness has long since disappeared, replaced on both sides by appreciation for a very loving connection. On Mother's Day Jennifer is wont to write personalized notes to her girls, telling each of them how wonderful they are in their own way. In return, when Cindy took them all to a spa, the girls left love notes to Mom on her breakfast tray every morning.

Finding the right boundary for her financial generosity to her mom and sisters is sometimes a struggle for Cindy.

"My mom never had two nickels to rub together, so dealing with money is kind of an issue for me," Cindy says openly. "I don't know what's enough and what's not enough to give. I want to help, yet I don't want to change her standard of living, because something could happen and I wouldn't be able to keep it up."

But when it comes to giving emotionally, Cindy never thinks twice. A few years back when Jennifer had extensive abdominal surgery, Cindy rearranged her brutal schedule to come home for ten days and do her stint nursing her mom.

"I was all bent over," Jennifer recalls, "and Cindy would put me in the tub and bathe me like I was three—or ninety. I don't know which. My new husband was just amazed. He said he could never do those things for his mom."

"Well, Mom, it gave me a chance to get a good look at you naked," Cindy kids her. "Every time I come home I make sure I get a chance to see you naked, because I want to know what I'm going to look like when I get older. So far I have nothing to worry about. The boobs are still good!"

Louise Nalli and her daughter, Jacqueline Nalli

Do you *love* your mother, Jacki?

"Yes, without question."

Do you *like* your mother?

"Well . . ." There is a long pause. "My mother is the obstacle from whom I have learned everything. I have pushed, shoved and fought my way through this relationship and we are still trying very hard to become friends. If I could, oh my God, find harmony and peace of mind with her, it would enhance all other things in my life. We just can't seem to unlayer all the old stuff between us."

And how do you feel about Jacki, Louise?

"She is everything to me. I would do anything for her, but I know that she resents me. She thinks I do too much."

. . .

Like so many mothers and daughters, Louise and Jacki each want what the other cannot give.

Louise expected her daughter to fill the huge hole in her heart created by an unloving family and a lackluster marriage. "I never had a doll as a child. When Jacki was born I felt I finally had something that was mine to love and take care of. She says I'm controlling and manipulating and overprotective. But I can't help it. She's all I've got. I wanted to expose her to everything I missed. Only the best. Piano lessons. Dancing lessons. Skating. Cotillion. Private Catholic school.

"Jacki is a very compassionate person. If she makes five cents she'll give ten away and she is very good to me in material ways. But I miss the personal, emotional things. I guess it's my fault. Nobody ever showed me any affection. My father abused me and my mother looked the other way. If you don't see affection, you don't know how to pass it on."

For her part, Jacki just wants her mother to stop trying to control her life and let her be.

"Even as a child, I wanted my independence and she wanted her authority. I am forever resisting her in a fight for my identity and I'm ferociously resentful. It's rare that she recognizes me as I am. She projects her image of what a Jacki should be—someone more open, more conventional. The Jacki that exists doesn't need her protection, but she can't see that. So I wear this nice armor with Teflon on the outside so she can't stick to anything."

Do. Do. Do. Louise can't do enough. Jackie feels smothered. If Jackie casually says she needs curtains for her kitchen, her mother arrives with a catalogue full of paper-clipped pages and says: I'll buy these for you, depriving her of the opportunity to make her own choice. Jacki, a practicing Buddhist, runs a nonprofit foundation she established to aid impoverished children in India and Nepal. If she happens to mention to her mother that she's swamped with paperwork, Louise immediately offers to come over and take care of it. If Jacki complains of a headache, Louise, who is a registered nurse, prescribes a medication, badgers her to see a doctor and may even make the appointment.

"I know I'm hypervigilant," Louise says, shrugging her shoulders. "Jackie is completely capable, but I worry about her constantly. And I know it's wrong for a mother to be that way. I read all the books by Bradshaw and Buscaglia and I'm trying to change. But she's mine, and I don't want anything to happen to her."

Jacki admits her mother's love is "constant and heartfelt. As stubborn and crazy as I've been, she is always there." That revelation came to her after decades of withholding, and it triggered the ponderous attempts at closeness that have engaged them in recent years. When they aren't rubbing each other with emotional sandpaper, they visit museums, exchange books, shop, go to movies and meditation classes. One of Jacki's fondest memories is the Thanksgiving dinner Louise created for an enormous number of her friends. It's only when they stroll back in time that it becomes painfully obvious why they can't cut the rope that ties them to their old hurts.

Louise plaintively tells Jacki, "I would like you to call me Mom or Mother, instead of Louise."

"I can't," Jacki responds.

"In what way wasn't I a mother? I was there. I fulfilled your needs. I loved you. I just don't understand."

"You don't have to understand," Jacki sighs. "If all my needs were filled, I wouldn't feel like I do. I was robbed of my childhood. I was a latchkey kid surrounded by adults. You didn't treat me like a child; you treated me like an adult, so I had to become one. Do you know another eight-year-old who vacuumed and did everything in the house?"

"I did to you what was done to me. That's how I felt when I was a kid. I was never myself." Louise shakes her head sadly. "But you seemed so happy. You went to nursery school. You had friends. I have the movies of your birthday parties."

"It wasn't all bad, but when I came home, you weren't there."

"I do feel guilty about that, but it was only for an hour and a half, and where I worked was just across the alley."

"Yes, but in a child's mind, that's a long time. And when you were home, all you talked about was your work. So I created my own private world where I was happy, but you'd never let me alone in it. You've just never let me alone. You never got to live your life. It was put on you by others. And my struggle is just to live my life my way. We're two people trying to do the same thing from completely different perspectives."

Louise is silent. She looks down and says, "But you know I love you. You are my life."

"And I love you," Jacki answers calmly, "because you have yourself. You are who you are, not because you have me."

Louise beams. "Oh, I'm on cloud nine. That's the first time I've heard you say the words 'I love you.' I've seen the actions but never heard the words."

Jacki nods in her cool, serene way. "I wish I could put aside my anger and say this with great joy. I wish when I hugged you it didn't feel like you wanted something."

"Well, I do," Louise says. "I want you to hug me back."

Jeanette LoPiccolo and her daughter, Maria Busciacco, and her daughter, Deanna Busciacco

They form a three-generation assembly line to prepare the stuffing. Jeanette, the eighty-one-year-old grandmother, wipes the eight pounds of mushrooms with a towel. "You can't wash them in water," she explains, "Not good for the texture." Deanna, her twenty-one-year-old granddaughter, cuts them up while her mother, forty-five-year-old Maria, sautés them with garlic and oil. "Then," Maria describes, "I mix the mushrooms with the insides from three round Italian dome breads. I don't like to use cubes that come in a package. After I break the bread into little pieces, I add six pounds of sausage that Mom and Deanna have skinned and broken up and I've already cooked. All that goes together with two eggs, one bag of cooked rice, one-third of a bunch of chopped parsley and a half pound of locatelli."

This is the stuffing Maria's mother, Jeannette, fixed when *she* was growing up. And this is the recipe Maria's daughter, Deanna, will someday follow, hopefully with her own daughter by her side. The ties that bind the women in this family are made of kitchen string.

And they are never so binding as before every Thanksgiving and Christmas, when you will find the three of them gathered at Maria's home to cook the holiday meal. Maria, a stout, feisty matriarch whose life—like her mother's before her—is totally devoted to her family, stands by her command post, the stove. In the twenty-five years since Maria left home to marry, she has never lived more than five blocks away from her mother in a tightly knit Italian neighborhood.

"Until it got hard for my mother to walk," Maria says, "she was at my house every day and she could never sit still. She did my washing. She loves to iron. I'm very fortunate."

Jeanette, the wrinkled four-foot-eleven-inch object of her daughter's obvious affection, sits in front of a cutting board, knife at the ready. "I couldn't do my

share this year," she says apologetically. "I used to do more, but that was before my arthritis."

"Mommy, you're eighty-one," Maria declares. "You're allowed to rest now." She pours a cup of coffee. "My memory of my mother my whole life is with a dust rag and a saucepan. I came home from school for lunch, it was already on the table for me to put in my mouth, and she was either cooking for dinner that night or cleaning. I said I'll *never* be like this. Then you get married and you do the same thing your mother did."

"I never taught her how to do anything," her mother interjects. "She was just there, thirteen or fourteen years old, hanging over the pot, watching. That's how I learned from my mother and how she learned from her mother."

Now it's Deanna's turn to hang around and watch. For the last several years she's been assigned to get up at 5 A.M. and put the stuffed turkey into the oven to free the space for everything else that will have to be baked or warmed later. It's a pattern dating back to when she was three years old and woke up one Thanksgiving dawn with an earache. "I went downstairs to sit in the kitchen, where Mom was sewing up the turkey. She gave me some juice, and I just started getting up every year because I liked to be with her.

"Finally, when I was a teenager she said to me, 'I'm not getting up anymore. It's *your* job now. Here's where everything is. You put it in the oven.' Now I don't have to wake up to do it, because I'm usually just coming in from a club."

Comes Christmas, the menu is even more elaborate. Caesar salad, scarpels (crepes filled with grated cheese, parsley and black pepper rolled tight and served in chicken broth), shrimp scampi, a whole filet of beef, a crown roast of pork stuffed with mashed potatoes, sausage and mozzarella, shiitake mushrooms, snap peas, and a variety of pastries for dessert. And that's just for Christmas Day. There's a separate menu for Christmas Eve.

The kitchen ritual is even more frenetic. This year, because Jeanette's arthritis kicked up, they decided to eliminate her renowned crab cakes from the traditional seven fishes served on Christmas Eve. But the pain in her gnarled hands didn't prevent her from helping prepare the 150 manicotti. Jeanette whips up the batter, which she and Maria then fry, standing hip to hip by their individual pans, while Deanna, stationed nearby, mixes the ricotta filling. They lay the crepes to cool on the kitchen table protected with brown paper, and everybody sits down to stuff and roll.

Their table talk isn't particularly intimate—mostly gossip or a barb about cutting a vegetable too thick or an offhand remark that sparks a piece of family history. "When you were born, Deanna, you were premature" is one of Maria's favorite tales. "You weighed three pounds thirteen ounces and nearly died. I couldn't bring myself to go to the nursery unit to see you because I was so afraid to lose you. Your father went, though, and said you were the most beautiful baby ever born. I finally walked to the nursery and nearly fainted. You were like a piece of ground meat to me. Skinny legs. Patches on your eyes. Tubes up your nose. And so much hair. You were the only baby who wasn't bald. And your father had the nerve to say you looked just like me!"

What binds these mothers and daughters isn't what they say; it's the women's work they do together, especially those domestic traditions centering on holiday meals. This is their recipe for love.

"We don't talk about how we feel," Jeanette says, "but we know what's there. Daughters are so different from sons. Boys marry. They have their own family they get attached to. You don't see them as much; you don't talk every day like with a daughter. You know that old saying: A son is a son till he takes a wife; a daughter is yours for all of your life."

Janet Leigh and
her daughter, Jamie Lee Curtis

"*I* don't like the way that cough sounds, Jamie. You've had it too long."

"I know, Mother."

"There's a wonderful new antibiotic called Cipro. It cured my husband when he had all that junk deep down and couldn't get rid of it."

"Yes, Mother, you told me."

"Cipro. C–i–p–r–o. I want you to ask your doctor about it."

"Uh-huh."

"C–i–p–r–o." Janet spells it again. "You're not going to do this, are you?"

"Mmmmm."

"I know you're not going to listen."

Jamie Lee Curtis throws her hands in the air in mock despair. "Oh, Mom, get *over* it." Like most daughters, she has no intention of taking her mother's advice.

Away from the glare of the klieg lights, two of the most famous faces in Hollywood are nothing more than the sum total of the labels—"mother" and "daughter"—that Jamie playfully glues on their foreheads for a photograph. They have the identical body type—slender and taut—although Jamie is slightly taller; the same beautifully etched lips and huge, incandescent eyes—Janet's hazel to green, Jamie's navy blue—defined by long lashes that look like they come from a box, but don't. When a bare-shouldered photo was discussed, Jamie protectively nixed the idea. "I would not do that to my mother. Women of a certain age should not be photographed with their shoulders exposed."

They are easy with each other in a comfy, cozy way that suggests there are no unfinished issues, no competitive undercurrents. "There is this misconception," Jamie points out, "that celebrity mothers are somehow excused from normal motherly behavior. My mom was never a celebrity to me. She worked—and her job was movies. She came to May Day and Christmas Fair at school like everybody else. I never thought she was glamorous. She was usually wearing tennis clothes. I did think she was always very natural and beautiful, which she is

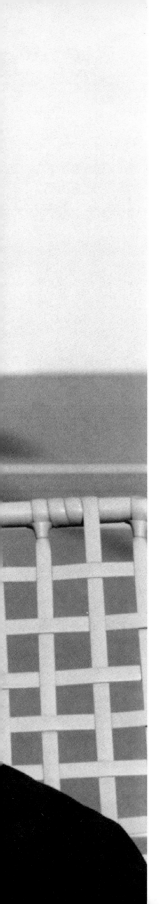

to this day. What was particularly hard in our situation—where my mother was famous very young—was that I was famous just for being born and then famous as I became an actor. But I don't ever want the basis for our relationship—or how we communicate—to be about her coming to one of my openings. Or me honoring her on a podium when she gets an award. We are so much more than that. I don't look at our relationship as something to chat about on *Oprah*. Actually, having to deal with my parents in a celebrity light is the least favorite aspect of my entire life. It feels phony. It's more important for me to value her for who she is. I actually call her Jeanette Heller, which is her maiden name."

Janet neither "encouraged nor discouraged" Jamie from a film career. "You can't direct your children's future. They have to follow their own lead. I just said I wished she would, at least, finish high school." *That* piece of advice Jamie followed, but she quickly dropped out of college. "I was not a scholar. I had no business being in college. I just wanted to get one gig, then another one. And I got unbelievably lucky."

Jamie, the second of Janet's two daughters, is recalled by her mother as "a spirited, independent, mischievous child."

"How about 'obnoxious' and 'hyper'?" Jamie suggests.

"Well," Janet responds gently, "it *was* a challenge to find the balance between squelching you and giving you too much rein. It's certainly easier for us to be friends now that the role of disciplinarian is gone. I don't think it's a parent's place to tell a grown child that she disapproves of something."

Jamie nods. "I will say I have never had a mind trip placed on me by my mom. And I've never felt smothered by her."

"I very consciously knew I didn't want to live my life through my children," Janet says. "The one problem I had with my mother, whom I idolized, was that she never created a life of her own. And that's a tremendous load on a child. I want to be part of Jamie's life, but not intrusive."

There are no taboos on what they discuss, and when they hit an impasse that a conversation can't handle, they write letters. "When the end comes, which is something I can't even think about," says Jamie, "we will have already said everything that needs to be said. And we will have always told the truth to each other."

One thing they rarely talk about is their craft. Jamie says she didn't learn much from Janet about how to act but what she did get was more valuable. "My mother showed me how to be a professional. She has a very strong professional credo. One of the biggest land mines for any actor is ego, because they are always being told they're hot stuff. My mother recognized that she was very fortunate to have this wonderful job and, therefore, should not be demanding. Just do your work and have a good time. She never told me these things but from observing her I understood the idea of being equal with everybody else in the workplace."

Once she starts on why she admires her mother, you can't slow her down. "Look at this woman. The Cinderella story of her life and the shifts she has experienced: two marriages, one long and committed; raising two daughters, an author four times over and a remarkable career as an actress. She has navigated an absolutely brutal industry—particularly brutal to women—and played in all the places you can play as an actor and nailed it every time. I have a very self-sufficient mother. I just keep thinking about her survival skills. You are tough as nails in the best sense of the word, Mama, and you've still managed to hold on to who you are: a very real, lovely woman.

"Moreover"—she pauses dramatically—"I must give credit where credit is due. You are the world's greatest organizer. Closets. And traveling. She has these sheets of paper and if it's a business trip in the summer for two days, she can pull up a sheet that says one dark suit, one light suit, two pair light hose, one pair low heels, don't forget tennis shoes. Da . . . da . . . da. This woman is astonishing. This is the inherited gene I am most proud of."

Janet has gone from blushing at Jamie's praise to laughing at herself. "But you have surpassed me. After the year you gave me the labeler for Christmas, you bought me the laminator so I could coat all my papers and speeches and I didn't even know such a thing existed.

"I so much admire Jamie's capacity for love. Just one little example: We have this ritual on my birthday or Mother's Day where Jamie comes over with a box and says, 'You can't look.' We go upstairs and she makes me close my eyes and she dresses me in a dress or pants outfit or whatever she's bought and she says, 'Okay, open your eyes now,' and it's always something just wonderful."

Jamie also has her own birthday tradition. "Every year on my birthday at 8:36 A.M. I call my mother and I do this." She begins to mimic a birthing coach. " 'All right, Janet. Come on. Keep pushing. Come on. Breathe in. Breathe deep. It's okay. There you go.' For a minute I cajole her and when my clock says 8:37 I start to wail like a newborn, and I thank her for pushing so hard. And she laughs and then she cries. Whenever I see someone on her birthday I make a point to ask her, 'Have you called your mom today and said thank you?' "

Adah Askew and her daughter, Jill Bargonetti

J ill and Adah sit cross-legged on the floor, facing each other, ready to talk. It had taken over a year and a half for them to reach this confrontation. As with so many issues between a mother and daughter, the bricks had slowly piled up until the wall could no longer be ignored.

This particular wall began forming at Jill's wedding in New York. Adah, divorced and living in Hawaii, had flown home into a maelstrom of too many people and too much tension—including her ex-husband with a new wife who treated her presence like an intrusion. Unable to put aside her own angry feelings and nurture her daughter at a very stressful time, Adah flunked the "where is Mom when I really need her?" test.

Although Jill carried her hurt in silence, it couldn't mask the obvious erosion of the closeness they'd once shared. Even after Adah had moved back to New York, removing the physical distance between them, the emotional distance remained. Now Jill was pregnant, and Adah "wanted her to go into childbirth with everything clean between us." She phoned her daughter and offered to have a karma cleansing. "I needed to give her the opportunity to clear the air so that every time she saw me, she wasn't thinking about this thing that was separating us."

Karma cleansing is a technique used in a mystical self-development movement called Arica, to which Adah has belonged for some twenty years. She'd become a follower at age thirty-eight when she decided to end her teenage marriage to Jill's father, a white English professor. By then she'd completed college herself after ten years of night school and earned a master's degree in counseling. "It was a chance workshop in Arica that pushed me over the edge," she explains. "I realized how extremely dependent I'd been all my life. I knew I'd die if I stayed in my marriage. So I went off on a forty-day retreat and came home with my head shaved, completely bald. Most kids break loose when they go to college. I'd missed that and now it was my turn."

Adah embarked on what she now characterizes as her delayed adolescence just when her thirteen-year-old daughter, Jill, was entering the same stage of rebellion. "I guess you could say Mom and I went through our adolescence together," Jill says. "In the beginning, I was embarrassed by this free spirit she'd become, but then all my friends wanted to hang out with her because she was cool. I wanted to do what I wanted to do, and she wanted to do what she wanted to do—so we both got to do whatever we wanted. She traveled a lot and wasn't always around. She was pretty self-absorbed, but it was fine because it only made me more self-reliant. And sometimes I felt we had changed roles and I was the mother, giving her advice."

Both of them admit those were tumultuous and often trying years. "We certainly went through our craziness," Adah says. But they emerged as two strong, independent women with a great respect for each other. Jill is a Ph.D. in biology who's getting kudos for her cutting-edge cancer research at Hunter College. Adah runs a counseling program at an exclusive private school. The foundation of their relationship is a determined effort at open communication—something Adah had missed with her own mother and set out to create with Jill.

"My mother was never a person I could talk to or be honest with about my life," Adah says. "I very consciously wanted to provide that for my daughter." Clearly she succeeded.

"I was always comfortable with my mother," Jill says, "and could talk to her about whatever was going on in my life. Growing up in the inner city is hard. I had girlfriends who got pregnant and dropped out of school; guys who got involved in heavy drug use and died. None of them could talk to their parents. I never had that problem. I never felt she wasn't there for me."

Except at the wedding.

They sit quietly, hands in their laps, making contact, left eye to left eye, an Arica ritual that followers believe opens the soul to truth. Jill does all the speaking. Adah's job is to listen but not to respond, to simply give her daughter a nonjudgmental space to dump the baggage that had come between them.

For over a half hour Jill talks. "I needed you emotionally and I hated that you weren't there for me," she begins. And as she spells out the litany of wrongs she'd felt from her mother at the time of the wedding, she lets go of the strings holding her hurt and it floats away.

Afterward they kiss and they cry. The business is finished. Their karma is cleansed. Now they can talk about the good things between them.

"Who I am as a person, my strength, comes from what my mother gave me," Jill says. "I admire her ability to be true to herself. She has taught me to question. That nothing is ever completely cut-and-dried, which is so important to my career as a researcher. And she has shown me that I don't ever have to compromise. That I have the ability to do whatever I want. My mother had to deal with all kinds of racism when she married my father. Because of how she managed that, I can handle the racism I encounter as a young black woman in science. She's given me the example of how to relate to people of all races, nationalities and educational backgrounds."

Adah smiles, eager to return a compliment. "And Jill gives so much back to me. I value her maturity and her insight. She is my confidante. Not only my daughter but my good friend. I'm so proud of her accomplishments. I have no doubt that she will win a Nobel Prize for her scientific discoveries. And I expect to be in the audience."

Jill laughs. "Unless you're on another one of your trips!"

Ada Balmaseda and her daughters, Elaine Alatriste and Liz Balmaseda

Ada, *mamasita,* rest a minute. *Bastante* with the rice and beans, the cooking, the cleaning and the cha-cha-cha. Put away that ticket for your favorite gambling-day cruise to the Bahamas. Listen while your daughters tell of a hardworking, joyous woman who, in her simple way, is the gravitational force that holds the family together.

Can you do that, Ada? Or would it be impossible for you to take instead of give?

Ada Balmaseda comes from a family which, in typical Cuban fashion, is dominated by women. "My mother has five sisters and one brother," her eldest daughter, Liz, explains, "and the women are almost Amazonian in their strength. If you are a Cuban mother, you want to have daughters, because the perception is that girls will take care of you when they grow up. Boys won't."

"Oh, for sure," Ada agrees. While she also has a son, she's quite open about her preference. "For myself, I love the two girls."

In Ada's vocabulary, the synonyms for "love" are "protect" and "provide."

"It was hard when they were growing up," she remembers. "Very hard."

But there was nothing deprived about their life. Their house pulsated with bright colors and boisterous fun instigated by Ada, as she bustled around the kitchen, laughing, singing and swinging her hips as she stirred the pots. "Mom is a real party animal," says Elaine, the younger daughter. "She'd always be egging on the cousins to dress up like drag queens."

"She was a nightmare," Liz giggles.

And although Ada couldn't help her girls with their homework because she never mastered English, she made sure they did it. And did it right! She scrupulously attended every open house at school and even volunteered as a teacher's assistant. Later, to scrape up money for their tuition at a private Catholic school, Ada bought a minibus and started a business driving other girls to school, along with her own. "I didn't like them to walk," she says, ever practical.

41

"My mother was always persistent with us," Elaine says, "making sure we were the best we could be. She never let us slack off. Whatever we wanted to do, she would find a way to open that door. She even made all our clothes. It was a ritual to go to the fabric store with her, pick the pattern, pick the material. We always had to be chaperoned at dances and she would volunteer. Nobody ever minded, because she was the most fun mom to take."

She still is—only now she gets to go as a guest because Liz, a popular columnist for *The Miami Herald,* is on the A list for all kinds of celebrity bashes. "I love to take Mom to parties," Liz says, "because she has such a blast. She brings her camera and takes pictures of everybody."

"More than anything else," Liz rolls on, "my mother has taught me to be honest and genuine. To be myself. The first time I went back to my hometown in Cuba and I saw this place with unpaved roads where bathing meant dipping in a fruit can filled with water, I understood this is who I am. This is where I come from.

"My mother embodies the Cuban heritage of that little town and the essence of being down-to-earth. She never pretends to be who she isn't. She once slapped Gloria Estefan's butt in my kitchen. 'Ay! Ay! Gloria, you *eat,*' she hollered, and, bang, she smacked her butt like Gloria was one of the chicks she drove to school. Mom is my everyday reminder of how simple life is."

Liz and Ada and Elaine talk to each other several times a day. Ada has never been much on discussing her feelings, and while growing up, the girls confided more in each other than in her. "I was too busy in the kitchen to be their friend," Ada says. "That's the one thing I would do different. Be more their friend."

In her fifty-fourth year, Ada was diagnosed with breast cancer. "It was the darkest day ever in my life," Liz says starkly. "I thought cancer meant death. After the surgery she came to live with me for a while. The wound got infected. I would bathe her and everything. I was just numb."

Yet Ada never lost her optimism. She put her faith in her doctors and simply believed she'd be cured. "I had no education what cancer was," she says. "I felt when they took off the bad breast, that was the end of it. The cancer was gone. I never thought it would continue."

She drove herself to her radiation treatments and then went on to her job in a printing factory. "I felt better doing that. I didn't want to go home to think," she says. By the time the treatments ended, she had returned to cruising to the Bahama casinos again and living like nothing had ever happened to her.

If you talk to Ada today about cancer, she'll only tell you that she's too busy worrying about Elaine to think about herself. That's because five years after Ada's mastectomy, breast cancer revisited the family and struck Elaine. Ada feels it was her fault, that she somehow gave it to her. Elaine was thirty-two, married with two little girls, aged one and three. But when she became ill, it was obvious that she was still and forever her mother's child.

"We put our house up for rent and moved into an apartment in Mom's building. She took care of my kids and made all our meals. She still does. I was so sick from the chemo that I couldn't bring myself to open the refrigerator. I never thought twice about who would help me. I knew my mom would. She's my mom. And she was also my inspiration. Seeing her so well five years after her treatment gave me hope. If *she* could do it, I knew *I* could."

Elaine holds an activist attitude that as long as she does everything medically necessary, she'll lick the cancer and be fine. She is pregnant again, awaiting the birth of a son. Yet in an all too familiar refrain she says, "It's my mother I worry about. Every day I'm still helping her get through *my* ordeal. She's always in a panic worrying about me. In the last few years, we have developed so much in common. Sharing breast cancer and becoming a mother myself has helped me understand my mother a lot better. I'm living her life, caring for my children like she did for us. And it's a good life. I hope I can have as much fun at sixty as she does.

"It's funny. When she went through her cancer, I never thought of her dying. I knew she'd pull through. But when I got sick, I actually came to the realization that I wanted to go first. It would be much harder for me if she wasn't here. I don't know if I could survive without her."

Liz feels pretty much the same way. "My mom helped me survive my divorce," she insists. "I was so afraid to tell my family. I was so sure I'd get the typical Cuban line, how the streets are hard; don't let him go. But my mother shocked me. She said, 'That s.o.b. You deserve better. You don't have to take his crap.'"

Both sisters admit that their mother still thinks they are her little girls.

"Sometimes that's completely comforting," Liz says.

"And sometimes it feels controlling," Elaine adds. "When I was going through chemo and all my surgery I needed someone to control my life and I was glad Mom was there. Now she has a problem backing off, so I just blow up and tell her, and usually she listens. Still, of all the mothers I know, I wouldn't have traded this one for any of them."

Nor would Liz.

In 1993, when she won a Pulitzer Prize for her newspaper columns, the invitation to the awards luncheon in New York included one guest. "There were only two people I could take: my mom or my then husband. And I said this honor is for me; it's not part of my marriage, and I want the memory to always be mine. In my heart the only honest thing was to take my mother because she'd be in my life forever. She won't fly, so we went by train from Miami, and it took forever. I wanted to make it a nice trip for her, so I got a suite at a lovely hotel and we stayed a week. I kept wanting to take her to Fifth Avenue to shop, and she only wanted to go to Chinatown and buy designer knockoffs.

"The luncheon was one of the greatest days of my life. There's my mom, a factory worker, sitting at this major table with all these glittery figures and she was so proud, even though she was embarrassed she didn't speak much English. It was right to have her with me. It wasn't just to say thank you. It was to acknowledge that I wouldn't have been there, I wouldn't have won a Pulitzer, if she hadn't put all that effort into me for all those years."

Some might say the Balmasedas' relationship needs more air. They would argue that their closeness is the oxygen that sustains their lives.

Janet Hauerken and her daughter, Michelle Fryman

"Who else can hurt you as much as someone that you care about so very deeply?" Janet asks, speaking from the pain in her heart, which is reflected back in her daughter's eyes.

If, as it is often said, love and hate are flip sides of the same coin, then Janet and Michelle should be millionaires. They are either smoldering with anger or attached like Velcro. Both complain they're sick to death of fighting, but they've become so skilled at hurting each other, they don't know how to break the pattern.

In one breath Michelle can say, "I have always been afraid of my mother. Nothing I ever did is good enough. She can tell me my dress is too short or too tight, and I come completely undone. Anything I do or say is taken the wrong way. Sometimes I feel I have to pay for her miserable childhood the rest of my life.

"Ever since I became a teenager, there's been this competition, like she didn't want me to be attractive or popular. I remember when my parents divorced, I had graduated from college and we went out to a bar together and guys my age were dancing with my mom. She's a very attractive woman. And she was like, hey, they like me better than they like you. I felt so cut by that. It was so mortifying that I stopped going out with her. The last thing I'm going to do is give her more opportunity to hurt me. I'm just going to go away. That's how I am."

But then Michelle will flip-flop and lovingly say, "My mother was the only person who supported my going to college. I was very shy and I was scared to death and I only got through it because I knew she loved me. Mom's had a really hard life. She didn't have my opportunities in terms of being able to make her own choices, like going to nursing school the way she wanted. But I'm so proud of her. She started back to college when she was almost fifty, and I thought that was great. I feel so sorry she's been through so much and I want to make up for

that. Nobody has really taken care of Mom, really loved her the way she deserves. I want to make her not hurt anymore."

Janet is equally mired in contradiction. "When we're not hurting each other, I consider Michelle my best and dearest friend," she says. "We have a lot of similar interests. We enjoy spending time together. But she has the power to wound me just as I have the power to wound her. She can deliver some cutting or demeaning put-down, and after she's dropped this bombshell, she'll flounce out of the room and doesn't want to deal with it. She runs away from confrontation, and I don't know how to overcome that."

Their need for one another is as deep as the Grand Canyon—and just as impossible to fill. Oddly enough, the stories they tell of the wounds they've inflicted on each other are almost exactly alike. Just listen.

Michelle's Florida story: "There are many times when I just need to hear my mother's voice and I can't get hold of her and I get really upset." With her hand, she swabs the tears that keep interfering with her words. "Like the time I was in Florida for my brother's wedding. It was wonderful, but when it came time to leave, there was a big confusion around checking out of the hotel, and by mistake, my mom was waiting somewhere else to say goodbye to me before I went to the plane. I kept waiting and trying to call her and she didn't come. She didn't come! She didn't come! What I didn't know was that the hotel told her we'd already checked out. Here I am thinking my mother has abandoned me. She doesn't love me enough to say goodbye and I was hysterical crying. Where is my mother? Where is my mother? And the whole time she is somewhere else thinking: How could my daughter leave without saying goodbye to me?"

Janet's funeral story: My father was a very important figure to all of us—more like a father than a grandfather to Michelle. When he died, I don't think I ever felt so alone in my life. There wasn't anybody to hug me and I was afraid to be alone. I knew Michelle was grieving, too, but I needed her and she wasn't there for me. I couldn't take any comfort in her. It was like she had a sign on her that said: Keep off; don't touch me. And when I wanted to hug her, she didn't put her arms back around me. And then she delivered this really cutting remark about it being my fault the airline reservations got screwed up, and I went crazy. Just ballistic."

Janet is softly weeping as she speaks. "I was so disappointed because I needed her so much then. I just felt that moms never do anything right. No matter what I do, where I go, I'm supposed to be this wonderful, loving person who never makes mistakes. That's a really high pedestal to be put on. Nobody can exist up there. I was angry, upset, grieving for my dad. And I just cracked. And after all this, Michelle tells me she wants me to make plane reservations for her to come home for Christmas. Well, I didn't want to see her. I hated her at that moment. I couldn't stand to look at her. What kind of relationship do we have if, at a time like this, we hurt each other so much? I'm too damn old to play this game. We have these continual, perpetual misunderstandings. Whatever is making us crazy with each other has to stop."

Can a fifty-one-year-old mother and her thirty-year-old daughter put down their verbal weapons and make the peace they both desperately want? On this sunny afternoon, they've agreed to unpack their emotional baggage and examine it. Michelle rifles among her old stuff and digs out the recurring nightmare of her childhood. Sobbing almost uncontrollably at the memory, she tells her mother, "Oh God, it was so horrible, I was afraid to go to sleep at night. In the dream, I guess I'm eleven or twelve—not old enough to drive—and you and my brothers and me are driving somewhere on a big interstate. We go under a road and come up on the right—and you're not there. I don't know where you are, but you're gone. And I'm driving. I don't know how to drive and we're going to crash and I can't make us not crash. *I can't take care of us.* I'm so frightened. So scared. You're not there and I want you. I want my mother."

Janet is visibly shaken. She gathers her daughter in her arms and strokes her silky hair. "You never told me that dream. I can't imagine you'd think I was going to disappear from your life. I love you. I know you need me. I'm so sorry you felt so alone and abandoned. I can identify with that. I had the same feelings when I was a child. I was afraid of my own shadow. Somewhere along the way, I learned to fake it. To pretend in uncomfortable situations. I think that's what we do with each other. Instead of saying what's really important, we pretend everything is okay when underneath it isn't."

Michelle cuddles in her mother's arms like a child. "We have these big fights and we don't talk about it and it just lays there and we go on hurting each other instead of saying I'm sorry. Sometimes I'm so amazed I've hurt you, because I had no idea. You know it was really neat this morning when we had to shower at the same time and do our hair together. When I was a kid I thought you were the most beautiful person I'd ever known."

"I think you're gorgeous," Janet says. "And very special and I'm very proud of who you are."

Michelle sighs deeply. "Well, I am my mother—and that scares the hell out of me. I look like you. My body is like yours. I talk like you. My voice is the same. My face. My hair." And caught in the eternal dilemma of a daughter, she asks the unanswerable question. "And if I'm *you,* how can I be *me?*"

Ruth Bader Ginsburg and her daughter, Jane Ginsburg

*R*uth Bader Ginsburg's recipe for pot roast, as reconstructed by her daughter, Jane:

1. Brown a hunk of brisket in the reddish-orange cast-iron pot, given as a wedding present from someone who little suspected the rueful purpose to which it would be put.

2. Add carrots, celery, red wine, and simmer this mess for a very long time. (While simmering, drink some black coffee, read some legal briefs and tell one of your children to do his or her homework—for the third time.)

3. At the end of the protracted simmering, remove the former brisket and most of the carrots from the pot and puree the remaining contents— hereafter known as the sauce—in a blender.

4. Put the blend in the refrigerator long enough for the fat to rise to the top and congeal. (While waiting for this to happen, drink more black coffee, eat some prunes and revise the third draft you've demanded of Jane's English essay.)

5. After the fat has coagulated, remove all of it with a large spoon. (No fat must contaminate the dish. This is one of the few culinary commandments handed down by your mother, who never let a drop of fat disgrace her chicken soup—unlike the cousin who left great greasy puddles in her broth.)

6. Slice the former brisket, against the grain. (The memory of the roast ham with sliced thumb should serve as sufficient admonition to keep your fingers well out of the knife's path.)

7. Pour the purified sauce over the brisket slices and reheat in oven. Carry forth to groaning board. (And don't forget to heat—but not bake—the plates.)

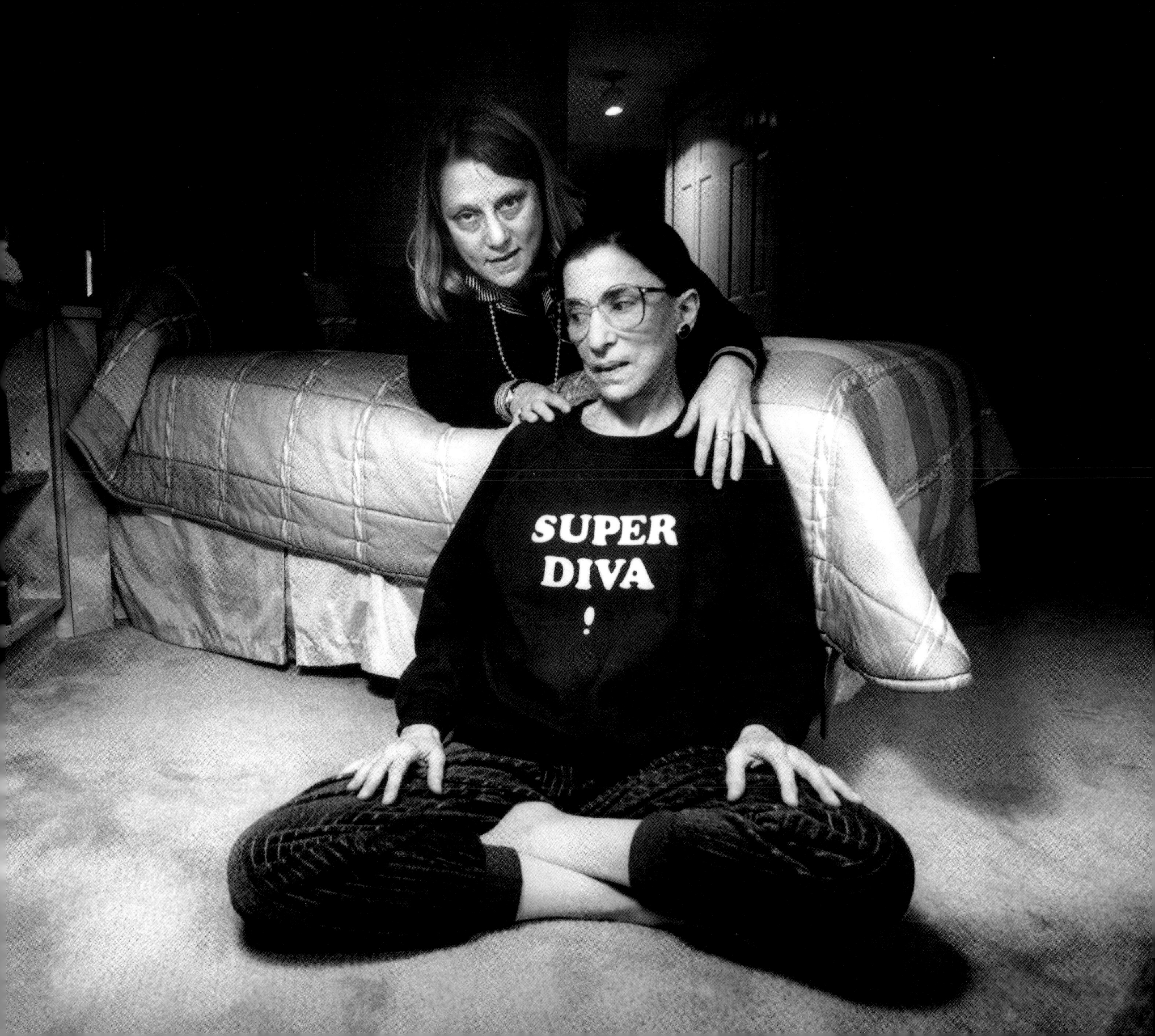
SUPER
DIVA
!

"Chillingly accurate," the Supreme Court Justice acknowleges, as Jane adds, "The kitchen was never one of my mother's zones of talent. Her episodes there were neither few enough nor far enough between." Frankly, Ruth thought that the quality of the dinner she prepared was less important than her being at home every night while they ate it—always to the strains of an opera or Beethoven symphony on the stereo. (Ruth's secret dream is to sing in an opera, although, in reality, she's a monotone who warbles only in the shower where no one can hear her.) What really mattered to this working mother was making certain that Jane got served massive portions of culture.

Ruth entered law school when Jane was fourteen months old and taught at law school after graduating when no law firm would hire her. "That's probably why I overcompensated on weekends," she says. "I schlepped Jane to every children's theater, to operas, Gilbert and Sullivan revivals, Rodgers and Hammerstein Broadway shows. I remember when she was about four I took her to a children's performance of *Turandot* and she stood up in the middle, screaming at the top of her lungs because she thought she could do as well as the soprano on stage."

Although Ruth taught Jane more about culture than cooking, her most important lessons were the example she set of how to be a successful and compassionate woman in a man's world. And the fortitude for that battle came from *her* mother. "My father was a sweet man," Ruth says, "but my mother had the real strength. Two of the things she instilled in me were to be independent and to be a lady, which meant don't get pregnant before you're married." A generation later, her independence assured, Ruth's admonishments to her daughter were more in the nature of standing up straight, cleaning her room and endlessly rewriting her English essays.

"In my defense," Ruth notes, "she has turned out to be a remarkably good writer."

Jane admits it took a long time for her to appreciate her mother's assiduous attention. "I was a resentful child and a spoiled brat. Mother is tremendously sentimental, but she could also be somewhat austere. When I did something bad, which happened often, my dad would yell, but my mother would be real quiet and I'd know she was very disappointed in me. Her searches and seizures of my childhood debris showed that Fourth Amendment principles held no place of honor in our household order," she says, winking.

"Thursdays, when she didn't teach class and worked at home, were my least favorite days, because the housekeeper was off and she was there to watch me. Mother has this tremendous tenacity. And while she has great compassion for others, she absolutely doesn't forgive herself. So when I was a little kid, I wasn't forgiven either, which was sometimes hard. I didn't appreciate then the high standards she imposed on me, but now I'm grateful, because I would have been quite lazy without them."

By and large, the things they once squabbled about are long forgotten, replaced by an admiring adult relationship that is deep, collegial and affectionate in a quiet way. In conversation, Ruth will unconsciously pick a piece of lint from Jane's sweater or reach up to stroke her shiny hair. Physically they are quite different: Ruth, petite and birdlike; Jane, taller than her mother and slightly stocky. But intellectually they're a perfect match. They take justifiable pride in being the first mother/daughter pair to attend Harvard Law School and the first mother and daughter to have both been appointed tenured professors at Columbia Law School, where Jane specializes in intellectual property rights.

They're too busy to shop together. The last time they can remember doing so was more than a decade ago, hunting for Jane's wedding dress. "We found it in the first store," Jane remembers, "and then we had to go everywhere else to be sure."

What they do more than anything else is talk—as might be expected of a mother and daughter who share the same profession, and a mutual respect. They discuss the law, books they've recommended to each other and articles they exchange because one thinks the other will find the content useful or interesting. For a long time Jane would voluntarily send Ruth drafts of her own writing. "I don't know at what point she began inviting my opinion instead of resenting it," Ruth says, "but now I mostly get reprints."

It was a great thrill but no great surprise to Jane when President Clinton appointed her mother to the Supreme Court. Way back in 1973—next to Jane's picture in her high school yearbook—she'd written under the heading AMBITION: "To see her mother appointed to the Supreme Court," followed by the words "will probably end up appointing her mother to the Supreme Court." To Jane, Ruth has always been an inspiration for what women can achieve. "I never thought I couldn't do anything because I was a girl and I never felt I missed anything because my mother worked."

And Ruth felt that being a mother meant that she never missed anything either. "What I bring to the judiciary are the many things that shape who I am," she says. "One is being female, one is being Jewish, and one is being a parent." The importance of her relationship with her daughter shows in the way her face softens when she relates this story.

"I will tell you something about us that touched me more than anything. Jane was in Paris when her son Paul was born and for a variety of reasons she was pretty miserable. She'd had a cesarean and was feeling physically awful. The baby was having trouble nursing and she felt rejected. It was not a good time at all. She called me from the hospital and we talked for two hours. I remember telling her that soon this baby will love you more than anyone in the world. And when we'd hung up I thought: Gee, I must have done something right as a parent. When my daughter was feeling really low, she didn't call a friend. She called me. She called her mother."

Greta White Calfe and her daughter, Verle Morning Star Sayler

reta White Calfe is the model of a self-sufficient woman. A widow with a wall of prize-winning rodeo ribbons in the fine house that she and her deceased husband built with their own hands, she has been named Indian Teacher of the Year and runner-up for Best Teacher in North Dakota. When she's not in her first-grade classroom, she operates a farm and cattle ranch on a windswept North Dakota plain. Just last night she brought a struggling newborn calf into her kitchen and nursed it with a bottle. Yet Greta insists that she couldn't manage on her own were it not for her daughter, Verle. "I rely on her for everything I do," she says. "I couldn't get along without her."

Verle Sayler is the model of a supermom. With four children—the oldest eleven and the youngest two—she decided at age thirty-nine to give up her busy practice as a chiropractor and enter medical school. Like her mother, she feels compelled to better the life of her tribe. "Mom has been pushing me for ten years to become a doctor. She has this education state of mind. And she's always been instrumental in raising my kids. My husband has been real supportive, too. But Mom and I, we cover for each other. I couldn't get along without her."

Together Greta and Verle are the model of a mother and daughter who could not stand alone if they did not have each other to lean on.

They were not always close. When Verle was five, Greta had to leave home to help support the family. "My husband and I farmed back then but we couldn't make enough to live on," she recalls. "He finally said, 'Greta, you have to go back to teaching. I'm losing three, four cows a month. I can't get ahead.' So I went back to work to make ends meet. By then the local Indian school had closed down and I couldn't get a job in the town because they had all non-Indian teachers, even though I had the same qualifications."

That was Greta's second bout with discrimination. When she graduated high

school in 1951, the local teachers college wouldn't accept her into their program. Because she was a Native American, they insisted she first give written proof that she could obtain a teaching job. Nearly a decade later, not much had changed. The only school that would hire her was hours and hours away in South Dakota. So for the next five years she was able to come home only one weekend a month.

"That's when I became a daddy's girl," Verle says. "Mom and I finally got to know each other when I was in the fourth grade and she started teaching at my school. That was cool. She was two doors from me all the time."

By junior high the whole family had gotten into rodeo, and would go off on outings every weekend. "Mom and I used to compete against each other, roping calves and barrel racing," Verle says.

"But you won more than I did," Greta reminds her. "Gosh, we had lots of fun. We would support each other. When she'd leave the chute, I'd yell, 'Go get 'em, Verle. You can do it!' "

"We didn't care who won just so we got the prize money."

"We were good friends," Greta goes on. "But we've become really close since my husband died thirteen years ago. After that we just clung to each other."

"When Dad got sick, I was living in Texas doing a chiropractic fellowship," Verle says. "He called Easter weekend and said I had to come home. He died from cancer August 13, and there was never any question I'd leave. We were raised to believe that nothing was more important than the family."

"My husband, Oscar, was the whole authority structure," Greta explains. "He was a very strong man and when he died we were faced with a lot of problems settling the estate. I hadn't ever paid a phone bill or an electric bill. I didn't know where anything was. That's when I started to rely on Verle. We didn't have anybody else but each other. The strong get stronger and the weak run. My son was kind of living his own life, so I feel really lucky I had a daughter. I guess a girl's just closer to her mother."

Selling the ranch was never an option. "My dad's grandmother, Rabbit Woman, owned this land when the whites came in the early 1800s," Verle says. "We would fight tooth and nail to the death to keep it." Instead the two women sold Oscar's 200 horses, kept the 170 beef cattle and leased out the farmland.

"To keep both our places going and have our jobs, too, we really had to work together," Verle says. "My family lived with Mom for five years. Then for a while we moved out to my husband's ranch twenty-three miles away. But it was hard for us to be far apart; we're used to being together. So we moved back."

But not into the same house. Verle's family built their own place on a hill about an eighth of a mile away. And she obsessed about getting her medical degree.

"I'd always had it in my mind," Verle says, "but the kids slowed me down and I kept putting it off. Mom and I had many heart-to-heart talks sitting by the fireplace. She really urged me to do it. She's been so steadfast about staying on the reservation and trying to get our people motivated. Health care here is really bad. There's one doctor for about 6,000 people and the turnover is horrible. People never see the same physician twice. I knew if I became a doctor, I wasn't going anywhere. This is my home. It's where Mom is. But it was such a big decision."

Her medical school is a six-hour drive, and unless the snow makes it impossible, Verle tries to see her family on weekends—very much like what her mother had to do when she was a child. Verle shrugs. "I turned out okay."

"We've just always worked as a team," Greta says. "Long ago we did chores together. Then calving and roping and the rodeo. Now we're raising her family together."

Verle fingers her thick hair. "Truly I couldn't do this without Mom's help," she says slowly. "I don't have a lot of women friends. I don't really need them, because I've always had Mom. Nothing could be bad enough that Mom couldn't get me through it."

Greta would say just the opposite.

Brenda Villa and her daughters, Christina and Amanda

Don't you look pretty!
What little girl hasn't grown up hearing that phrase over and over? How then can we teach our daughters that true beauty is not measured by what we look like on the outside, but by who we are inside? That our bodies, however flawed, are beautiful because they house our souls.

Brenda Villa is a fairly typical American woman in that she judged herself mainly by the image reflected in her mirror. Brenda suffers from a vision problem peculiar to females known as "fat eyes." Small in stature with large breasts, she relied on bouts of anorexia and bulimia to fight her imagined bulges. "When they amputated my breast because of cancer, I was completely devastated," she says. In her mind, she'd lost the essence of what it meant to be a woman. It took the unqualified love of her daughters to prove her wrong.

Brenda had just turned forty-five when a young friend of hers underwent a mastectomy. "We both had children the same age," she says, "and we thought nursing our babies would help prevent cancer. Here is my friend with one breast gone and I thought I'd better get a mammogram fast. All my life I'd been afraid to get checked. I had cancer in my family; it's in my genes, but I just didn't want to know anything. Now I had a responsibility to my daughters, so I couldn't ignore it."

Brenda had stopped nursing only six months earlier. She didn't marry until she was thirty-nine. And because of medication she had taken for a thyroid problem, she never expected to have children.

"Amanda was our honeymoon gift, a miracle," she says. "She was six weeks early and only weighed four pounds. The first time I nursed her in the hospital, thank heavens we got it on videotape." Two years later Christina was born. "I wasn't at all disappointed when I didn't have a son because I'd always wanted a sister, and now Amanda would have one."

The mammogram, taken three years later, was suspicious. The biopsy

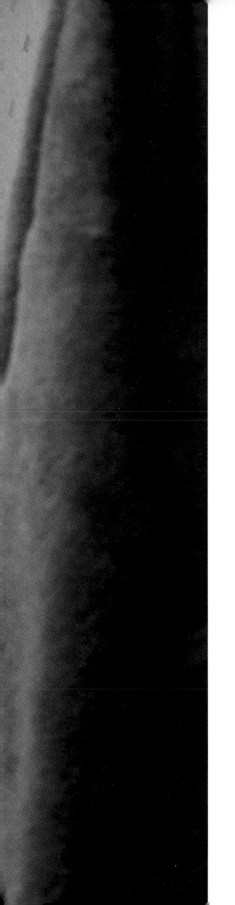

confirmed a cancerous tumor in the milk duct. "My first thought was that because I'd breast-fed both girls for so long I must have passed the cancer to them. But everybody assured me it can't be transferred. My second thought was: Please, God, let me raise them. Let me live long enough to get them right.

"I was desperate for what to say to them about the surgery. A woman from the Cancer Society said to talk about cancer being silly cells that weren't doing their job and the doctor would go in and take the silly cells away. I told that to Amanda, who had just turned five, but Christina was too little to understand. The night before the mastectomy Amanda wanted to see what the doctor had done to me when I'd gone for the biopsy. She'd cut the areola like a half-moon. When I showed her, she said, 'You've got a frown, Mommy. Doctor is going to take those silly cells away and make you a happy face.' When I got into the operating room I asked the doctor if she could make my scar turn up on each end like a smile, and when I woke up in my room, she'd drawn a huge smiley face on my bandage for Amanda to see when she came to visit me."

But what Brenda faced when the bandage came off made her ill. "It was so traumatic that I fainted. I didn't want my husband to see the scar, but he walked into the room, lifted my gown, kissed me and told me I was beautiful."

She stops speaking and wipes her wet eyes. Despite his complete support, Brenda still felt disfigured. "When I looked in the mirror, all I saw was horror. One side of me was bulging; the other was concave. I was so big and so lopsided. I just knew I couldn't go through life with one breast. I decided three months later to have the other breast removed as a prophylactic measure."

But now she felt even more deformed and went to great pains to hide her body from the daughters she'd so joyfully fed at her missing breasts. She no longer allowed them in the bathroom with her and carefully covered herself in their presence. Until one day Amanda innocently broke the rule. "I was drying myself after a shower when she burst in for something and caught me. I immediately covered my chest with my arms and turned my back. She walked over, put her little hands on my hips, turned me around and pulled me down to her. I had no idea what she was doing. She reached her arms up to me and said, 'Mommy, can I kiss your boo-boos and make them better?' Then she kissed both my scars and I just stood there and cried. The look on her face was not the disgust that I felt— but a look of warmth and love.

"That was the beginning. Now not a day goes by that both my girls don't kiss my boo-boos, with my clothes on or without them. They have helped me to rediscover myself. I used to run half-marathons and I've started to jog again. I planted a garden because I wanted to see something grow. I want life around me. I still find it hard to be in public. I have these protheses but I'm trying to get used to liking myself enough that when I go out I don't have to wear them. I don't feel comfortable yet. I still think everybody is staring at my chest."

Brenda prays that she can give back to her girls the amazing gift they don't even know they've given her. "I only hope from this experience that I can convince them to just enjoy the way they look without getting caught up in it like I did. Let it be what it is, but not who they are.

"By accepting me when I was so ashamed of my body, they have given me the freedom to accept myself. Every time they kiss my boo-boos, they help me to love *me* as a scarred person. In my heart, they are my healers."

Yasminka Rukavina and her daughter, Tatjana Rukavina

"Sac-ri-fice. Ach, I hate that feeling." Yasminka says in her thickly accented English. "I do only what I want. And the things what I do for Tanya, I do for both of us. She is part of me. I never think I am not getting something for myself. My duty is to give my daughter chance for her own life. Yes, I leave my career in Bosnia. But I have more important career: my daughter. Mothers should be mothers, and everything you do as a mother is from love."

In 1991, her daughter, Tanya, was thirteen years old and a budding artist when the war in Bosnia exploded at their front door and redesigned the map of their lives. Tanya's father, a composer, had dropped dead from a heart attack when she was only six months old. Yasminka managed to support them comfortably as a lawyer for the Bosnian government. Their cultured, joyful, middle-class lifestyle whirled around art, dance and music lessons, concerts and theater.

"My mother is a very strong woman. I never feel I miss anything growing up," Tanya says. "She always tell me some kids, like me, are different; they don't have fathers, and that's how it is. In our apartment in Sarajevo we have a huge bed we sleep in together when I'm little. She always wants to hug me and hold my hands. I feel we are friends."

The "friends" were awakened one night by the loud noise of fighting in the street outside their apartment. "Lock your door and don't open it," was the only help the police could offer. The Serbs had taken control of their district in Sarajevo. Tanya and Yasminka had suddenly become the enemy. No matter that they were nonbelievers, their family name and heritage stamped them as Muslims. And according to the ancient hatred of the Serbs, they were to be ferreted out and extinguished. For three days they cowered inside in fear, watching the snipers through the curtains and praying that Serbian soldiers would not beat down their door.

"It was like the movies," Tanya says. "These big expensive cars with Serbs in them going around, windows down just a little bit so you could see the guns. You know if you go out, you'll be dead." On the fourth day of their confinement, they were able to telephone Yasminka's sister, who bribed three different cabdrivers to bring her to rescue them. "We only have minutes to get out," Tanya remembers. "I stuff into two plastic bags some things important to me—some books and poetry, a few pictures, some jewelry, my diary, my ballet slippers, jeans. And a piece of

chocolate cake. My mom said, 'You are crazy. What good will this be if we are hungry?' "

They carried away their memories but left behind their tangible history—valuable objects and worthless trinkets, the significant and the sentimental, and worst of all, the photographs that documented their lives.

For several months they subsisted on the charity of family and friends, until Yasminka, a proud and independent woman, elected to move them to a refugee camp in Croatia. At least there they would not be a burden or a risk to anyone sheltering them. While they adjusted to the deprivations of a refugee life, Yasminka could not accept the useless emptiness of their existence. No school for Tanya. No opportunity.

"Every day I tell my daughter, 'Just draw one picture. Do something. If you do nothing, there will be nothing.' All the time I worry she is not getting education. Only with good education can she better her life. Have more options. There was no chance here for good things. After one year, I start thinking maybe we go to United States."

"One day Mom asks: Do we want to come to America?" Tanya remembers. "Like friends, we discuss everything because two people know more than one. My mother is great because she never decides for me. She wants me to think for myself. She always gives me facts and says do what makes you happy. Don't worry about her. I know always she will support me, no matter even if I decide the wrong thing. But I don't want to put both of us in a bad situation. I realize we have no possibility to go back to our district in Sarajevo. No job. No education. We're just sitting here. 'Okay,' I said, 'let's go to America.' "

They arrived in Philadelphia on a ticket paid for by the National Refugee Center with $100 from a Bosnian friend and a suitcaseful of optimism. A mother and daughter, independent as the columns that hold up an arch and dependent on each other as the arch itself on its two columns. They had lost everything they owned, yet saved what little they needed: their determination, their humor and their self-respect.

Sometimes Tanya wished she'd come alone. "I didn't want my mom having this bad experience. I thought: I'm younger; I can go through it, but this is painful for her. I felt bad she had to live like this."

Bad was the shame of collecting welfare for eight months until Yasminka, the former Bosnian attorney, got hired as a salesclerk at Bloomingdale's.

Bad was having to accept the kindness of a minister's family who, for ten months, provided a rent-free room in their home.

Bad was the sneering disapproval of fellow immigrants who frowned on their raw ambition to get Tanya the best education.

Awful was the constant worry over money.

But *good* was having each other. Tanya stretches her arm around her mother's shoulder to demonstrate. "Some days Mom would say, 'Oh, I can't do this; how are we going to get through?' Then it was my role to say, 'Yes, we can; we can do *anything.*'

"Some days I come home from a hard day at school and I'm weak. I leave seven in the morning and get in seven at night from my babysitting job. I say, 'Mom, come hug me. Give me some energy.' Or she is tired and she say, 'Come, Tanya, give me some of your energy,' and we hug each other. We share our strength. We make jokes about our trouble, like when I'm cleaning houses to make money. And always we think tomorrow will be better."

They have not been disappointed. When Tanya finished high school she won a full art scholarship to Parson's School of Design in New York. Yasminka found she could transfer her job to a Manhattan branch of Bloomingdale's.

They live in a sparsely furnished, run-down apartment where Tanya's pictures decorate the walls and the halls smell of cooked cabbage. Tanya rides the subway to her classes, toting her bulky art portfolio and her dreams of becoming a successful painter or illustrator. Yasminka rides the subway to her dead-end sales job, toting memories of her law career in Bosnia and the loved ones she fears will forget her. But her dreams do not include going back.

"I remember when the war started in Bosnia," Tanya says. "We watched those refugees leaving their homes with nothing in their hands and my mom said, 'I could never survive that.' " She looks at Yasminka, her direct, black eyes glistening with pride. "But you don't ever know what you can survive until you have to."

Margaret Atwood and her daughter, Margaret Atwood

Margaret Atwood, the elder, is a shy woman, markedly prone to understatement, who equates the attention of strangers with her loathing of formal tea parties, shopping for party dresses, cooking, dusting knickknacks and polishing silver. Should you ask her to talk about her incredibly accomplished daughter, the world-famous writer—fifteen novels, countless published poems, eleven honorary degrees, dozens of awards—Mrs. Atwood says impishly, "I didn't know Peggy was so incredible."

Well, how would *you* describe her?

"I would say Peggy is very satisfactory as a daughter."

Do you read her work? "I've read every word of every one," the mother replies without missing a beat.

"I think Mum wonders why there has to be so much language in my books," her daughter Peggy (as she's known in the family) interjects—only half joking. "I know Mum is very proud of me, but she never actually says anything about my work. Which is fine. I don't need to know what she thinks. She has her privacy. I suspect she would probably say the same thing she used to say when I went to a formal, which was 'You look very nice, dear!' "

"That's right," her mother answers on cue.

Not surprisingly, Margaret Atwood's parenting style reflected her less-is-more personal style. The essence of how she raised Peggy is easily summed up in the applesauce caper.

"I was about twelve and I wanted to make applesauce," Peggy remembers. "Mum didn't say to me you have to do it this way or that's not how you do it. She simply said, 'Fine. Go ahead and try it.' And she left me with my Betty Crocker picture cookbook to figure it out."

Margaret's recollection was a tad different. "I had to get out of the kitchen because it was such a mess." Still, it would never have occurred to her to intervene.

"A lot of parents are too intrusive," Peggy points out. "Mum was never very intrusive in my doings. Her main strategy was to get my brother and me busy with something on our own, so she could do whatever she wanted, which was usually to be outside. She was a great gardener, very physically active, and loved the outdoors. She took up figure skating at forty-seven.

"Her other strategy was to pretend to be really stupid. I would say, 'Draw me a bunny,' and she would say, 'Oh, I'm not good at drawing, you'd better draw me one.' "

Fortunately for her mother, young Peggy was a cheerful, contented child with a prodigious imagination who had no trouble entertaining herself. "I remember when her brother went off to kindergarten," Margaret says, "and I thought: What am I going to do with this child? She'll be so lonesome. I brought her home on the sled, and she took off her snowsuit and went around doing her little chores, putting her piles of junk here and there—and humming like a contented hen. I said, 'Peggy, you are having a nice little time singing,' and she said, 'Oh yes, I have lots of little hums like that running around inside my head.' "

The little hums ripened into elaborate long-running sagas invented by Peggy and her older brother, Harold, to amuse each other when they weren't writing and performing plays. By six, Peggy had written her first book of poems; the subject was rhyming cats. That was followed by a comic strip about flying carnivorous rabbits which gave way to a dress-designing phase in which she created elaborate pictures of clothes she dreamed of making.

"I don't thing Mother was so much encouraging of my interests as she was tolerant," Peggy says. "She was pretty much there and available, but she didn't interfere. Even when I announced at sixteen that I wanted to be a writer—and I think she was appalled—she only said, 'Well, how will you support yourself?' "

Peggy Atwood is the product of an unusual childhood. Her father was a forest entomologist, and in order to pursue his study of insects, their family lived more than half of every year in an isolated cabin, with no electricity, deep in the woods.

"I didn't spend a whole year in school until I was in eighth or ninth grade," Peggy explains. "We'd enter in late November and leave in early spring, usually in a different city. We moved twenty-five times in my first twelve years. In the forest, Mother would teach us in the morning, and if we finished our work, we could play. There was no form of entertainment. No movies, no theaters. Radio was unusual. Our toys were a set of wooden blocks that Daddy made and painted, some beads which were actually dyed macaroni and a huge assortment of stuffed animals. What we had were large numbers of books, and when it rained, you read or you drew. Mother always read to us at night. In one city her readings were so famous that all the kids in the neighborhood would come because their mommies didn't read to them. She let them stay as long as they were quiet."

The kinds of feminine pursuits girls usually learned from their mothers just weren't in Mrs. Atwood's lesson plan. "My mother was never interested in girl stuff," Peggy explains. "I guess whatever is denied to you is what you most want to investigate, so I went about acquiring domestic things outside the household. One of her friends taught me to knit and another how to crochet.

"She had zero interest in clothes, which, I suspect, is why we didn't have an adversarial relationship when I was a teenager. We never fought over clothes or deportment. She didn't even go with me to buy my first formal, though we did go to get the shoes dyed to match. It was like pulling teeth."

The one notable exception to Margaret's disinterest in the world of fashion and beauty was the daily ritual of doing Peggy's curls. Peggy had thick, unruly dark hair that begged for grooming, and every morning her mother would twist it around her fingers into perfect corkscrew curls.

"I would sit her on the table and get her a book. That's all I had to do," Margaret says, enjoying the memory. "She would turn the pages and I would read. I must say she learned to read very early. And as long as I was reading to her, she could tolerate my doing her curls."

"Or you could say," Peggy offers, "that literary activity means pain, but you can get through pain as long as you have literary activity. I couldn't get rid of those curls until I was twelve and Mum got busy with my baby sister. Fortunately my father couldn't do my hair because his fingers were too stubby. She still has my curls in a box in the cellar."

"I do, and I open it lots of times."

"Probably because you're looking for something else," Peggy kids her, in the genial banter typical of their conversation.

"Well, actually I'm looking to see if they have any moths in them," her mother replies. Margaret Atwood is not a woman who minces words.

"I probably got more of my intellectual side from my father," Peggy says, "but my life attitude came from my mother. The most basic thing I learned from her is that when you are fully depressed, what you need to do is go for a brisk walk.

"And the other thing I got is that it's more fun to have a good time than a bad time. She taught me to be strong-minded. To do what's right. To be very honest. But that doesn't mean telling somebody what you think of their dress. Mom has always been interested in things. Never been bored a day in her life. And," Peggy adds playfully, "she always pays her bills on time."

If you look for Margaret's influence in her daughter's novels, you'll find it not so much in the feminist themes as in the model she provided of a certain kind of woman—independent, self-sufficient, curious. At eighty-seven, Margaret insists on living alone and makes the concession of calling Peggy every morning at nine to let her know that she's made it through the night. Her mind is still as sharp as the spade she uses to turn her garden.

"If I have a reincarnation," she says, "I want to come back as an archaeologist. Just the other day I found a prehistoric arrowhead when I was picking stones out of my garden."

"Well, Mum, what if you come back as an animal instead of a human being?" Peggy asks.

"Then I want to be a loon. They're such beautiful birds. They live in water and can fly. They have parties and laugh. They have lots of fun springing over the water and singing at night. Yes, I want to be a wonderful loon."

Peggy listens to her mother with bemused affection. There is a sweetness in their byplay, in the way the adult daughter showers her mother with the loving tolerance that was so abundantly given to her.

"I once read an advice column," Peggy says, "about a woman complaining that her children never came to see her. The columnist wrote, 'That's probably because you didn't treat them well when they were children and they don't like you.' I said to Mum, 'See, you treated us well when we were growing up, and now we come around because we like spending time with you.'

"I really do like you, Mum. And I love you, too."

Laureda Byers and her stepdaughter, Alison Byers

Laureda Byers' introduction to stepmothering was a discouraging harbinger of things to come. Her husband's son and daughter from his previous marriage would come for their weekend visitation and, before bedtime, they'd all kneel down to say prayers. "Everybody would get mentioned in my stepdaughter Alison's prayers but me," she explains with a wry smile. "It was God bless Mommy and Daddy and the gardener and the nanny and Suzy and Emily and whatever, but I never made it into the prayers. It was obvious I was not part of the program. I was a nonperson. This went on for years, and I was never sure how I fit in."

When Laureda married Alison's father, it was quite clear that she'd bought into a package deal which included an active involvement with his preschool children. "No woman grows up thinking she's going to be a stepmother. That's not a life's ambition," says Laureda with a toss of her perfectly groomed bob. "I had never met a stepmother, so I had no idea how they were supposed to behave. And I'd never been a mother. So I had no idea how to do that either. Besides, Alison already had a mother. I knew I wasn't supposed to be a friend because I was an authority figure. And though I didn't have the title 'parent,' I certainly felt the responsibility. Unfortunately, I wasn't terribly demonstrative by nature. So I just sort of waited around for Alison to respond to me. She didn't—and for a long time I didn't do anything to change that."

For her part, Alison had little training in how to be any kind of daughter. She basically viewed Laureda, a successful entrepreneur with a career in business and marketing, as another piece of furniture in their elegant Georgian home. "I'd never really been expected to act like a daughter to a woman before," says Alison, a fresh-faced twenty-nine-year-old with a husky voice and a direct manner. "I was very much Daddy's little girl growing up. My mom was not a Band-Aids and Oreos kind of mother. She traveled for months at a time as professional photographer and I was raised mostly by maids and nannies."

When Alison turned fifteen, she stopped speaking to her mother altogether after a nasty confrontation involving stolen money and credit cards. At that point, it was decided that she should come to live with her father and Laureda, as her brother had already done. Six months later, her mother died suddenly from spinal meningitis without their rift having been repaired.

"It was the most horrible time," Alison recalls, wincing at the memory. "I was really a handful. Rebellious. Opinionated. Stubborn. I arrived with the attitude: 'Hi, I'm Alison and I'm trouble.'

"I'd decided I was totally unlovable and everyone hated me. For years I'd been living in New York, doing whatever I wanted: drinking, drugs, really walking on the wild side with little supervision. Now my mother's died and for the first time in my life I'm faced with my father and this woman he's married to, who are actively thwarting me; saying no, you can't do this or that. It never occurred to me that Laureda would be a warm, loving mommy type because in my experience women weren't like that. As far as I was concerned, she was superfluous. A distraction for my dad."

Laureda is one of those people who take their marriage vows very seriously. "I figured I'd married for better or worse, and when Alison moved in with us, I accepted that the bad times had arrived and that was part of the deal. It wasn't exactly unexpected. Early on I'd had a presentiment that she and her brother were needy and would demand lots of time and attention. That was the reason I'd decided not to have children of my own. I'd always had a full-time career and believed you can only do so many things well. Being the best parent that I could be to my husband's children was as much as I could handle and that was very important to me."

The possibility that Laureda might also be important to her was something Alison dimly sensed but, in the full throes of her teenage rebellion, would never have openly admitted. "I was totally devastated when my mom died. My reaction was panic. I had a

new family, a new city, new schoolmates. The whole world was scary. That's when, for the first time, I started to look at Dad and Laureda and say to myself: If I lose this chance, I lose everything.

"I certainly didn't show it, but somewhere I was becoming a little bit more invested in the concept of a normal family with this woman who was my dad's wife—but still not, in my eyes, anything like a stepmother."

While Alison was considering that she might actually buy into this idea, Laureda also had an epiphany. "After all these years on the sidelines, I finally said to myself: Laureda, you are the adult in this pairing and you have to take control. Like it or not, now that her mother's gone, we're it.

"I realized that it was my job to learn how to be emotionally demonstrative even if it meant practicing hugging until it felt natural. Underneath all her stuff, I could see this totally terrific girl who just needed a little remedial work. I felt I was lucky to have such an incredible person in my life, and I had the most to benefit if I could find a way to embrace her."

She set out to actively inject herself into Alison's life with mundane acts like insisting on a nightly sit-down family dinner, during which the kids usually ate in stony—and often stoned—silence. And in this family where emotional intensity spiked up and down like an EKG graph, Laureda developed a reputation as the voice of calm, consistency and reason. The sign that she'd finally achieved a primary role came when Alison—home on a college break—turned to her during an argument and matter-of-factly stated, "Well, I hate you and I've always hated you."

Great! thought Laureda. I finally matter. And to Alison's surprise she said, "That's really good, because at least we're being honest." Which is not to say she wasn't hurt. "But I knew that you can't build a relationship of trust until you're honest about how you feel. That really marked the beginning of what has become our wonderful relationship."

By her sophomore year in college, Alison was finally ready to grow up and stop hating everybody, including herself. "I guess," she admits, "I became willing to accept Laureda's view of me as a pretty cool person."

The pivotal event that closed their past and defined their future was Alison's twenty-first birthday party. "It was my first adult party and I wanted to go all out. Big and fancy.

"Laureda was very supportive and helpful. It was a multigenerational affair at a restaurant with a lot of old friends and family. When the toasts started, numerous people stood up and said all kinds of wonderful things about my mother, how proud she'd have been of me and how they wished she were here. I didn't think it would have been great at all if my mother had been there. She'd made me miserable for fifteen years.

"I was overcome with emotion, tears streaming down my face, and I got very defensive. I had this realization that somebody else had put up with all my bullshit for most of my life and we were forgetting about her. So it was very important for me to stand up and say, 'Hey, don't forget about Laureda. *She's* the one who deserves the tribute!' "

They both inhale deeply on their cigarettes, grinning at the memory of that evening. "It was one of the most divine moments of my life," Laureda says, "partly because it was totally spontaneous. I think part of the mother/daughter baggage is competition and we have no competition. We're just two people who welcome, delight and honestly applaud each other's successes.

"It was never for me to say that Alison was my daughter. That had to be her decision, not mine. But it worked out exactly how I wanted it. Alison *is* my daughter today. I couldn't imagine having a more amazing daughter in the whole wide world. And," she adds, patting her hips, "she didn't have to inherit my cellulite!"

Eleanor Cogshall and her daughter, Susan Erb

*L*ike every grandmother, Eleanor was always thrilled when her grandson came to visit. On that humid Fourth of July morning back in 1975, it was hard to say no to the precocious five-year-old who threw his arms around her knees and begged permission to cross the street to play.

"Be careful" were the last words little Cory ever heard.

Eleanor had to call her daughter, Susan, from the hospital to break the news that her child had been hit and killed by a car while he'd been left in his grandmother's care. "Susan later told me she believed that Cory's death was God's will," Eleanor says, "and I understood that meant she didn't blame me. But I was not on speaking terms with God and I will always blame myself."

Tragedy seemed to be stalking Eleanor. Two years earlier Susan's twenty-two-year-old brother had been felled by cancer after battling the disease since birth.

Here were a mother and daughter, both suffering the agonizing loss of their sons. But they could not comfort each other. Their pain had no voice, and its silence drove a wedge between them for almost twenty years.

"My way of mourning was to try to forget," Susan says. "I was divorced and had my daughter to think about. I got involved in a romance. I just tried to keep going and honor my son's memory."

By contrast, Eleanor, who'd always been the strong and capable one, fell to pieces and, at one point, attempted suicide.

"Understand that I was sixteen before I saw my mother cry," Susan says. "She was always very organized, made her lists and got on with things. That set a standard for a certain way of living, and now, when she wanted to act like a normal grieving person, crying and depressed, it was just so out of character. It made me uncomfortable and mad. Looking back, I think Mom wanted some kind of punishment from me. Maybe it would have been better if we'd had a confrontation."

Eleanor once asked Susan, "Why didn't you scream and holler and accuse me?"

Susan replied, "Because that's what you wanted—absolution and forgiveness from me. But when something like what happened with Cory happens, you can't blame anyone."

Mother and daughter tried to stay connected by doing things together—family parties, barbecues, trips here and there—while they concealed their enormous grief with small talk. "We cared enormously for each other, but we just didn't know how to talk about the impact of our loss," Eleanor says. "We chatted about everything else; we ignored what mattered."

As time passed, Eleanor managed to pull herself back into life. Raised as a Quaker and schooled as a social worker, she developed an activist volunteer career. Now it became Susan's turn to sink into despair and alcohol.

"My second husband had put a nice Band-Aid on my scabs from my losing my brother and son," she explains. "The end of our marriage ripped that scab off. I was just this big, moving sore. To top it off, my daughter, Tess, decided to go away to a boarding school not far from my mother, who began lavishing all this attention on her, and I felt really second shelf. It was incomprehensible to me that my mother didn't realize how bereft I was. Mothers are supposed to know these things."

"I didn't know how to break through to her," Eleanor replies. "For my own sanity, I had to cut myself off from her. She was destroying herself and I couldn't stop it."

"I was consumed by this horrible pain," Susan says, wiping her wet eyes at the memory. "Something inside me was so empty and I tried to fill it with sex and prescription drugs and booze. I can see now that I was trying to kill myself." And she nearly succeeded. The night before Tess graduated from high school, Susan had a drunken accident and ran her car into a tree.

"That's when I went crazy," Susan says. "My mother doesn't know this, because we weren't speaking at the time. I stayed in my house with the curtains closed. I didn't bathe or brush my teeth or wash my hair or go to the market. I lost forty pounds in two

months. When Tess came home on vacation I was wearing nothing but a Rolling Stones T-shirt. 'Mother, you are filthy. Just filthy,' she said to me. 'How can I respect you when you have no respect for yourself?'"

Tess's plea electrified Susan. She found the card of a psychiatrist that someone had given her and called him. "I realized there was something I did want to live for. My daughter."

Susan stopped drinking and committed herself to therapy. A year later, Eleanor invited her to join the family for a Labor Day visit. "It did not go well," Susan recalls. "Mother was rigid and I was rigid. The day I was to leave she said one of those typical mother lines like 'Why is it always *my* fault?' And I replied, 'Mother, there have been hurt feelings on both sides.' That was the icebreaker. I started to cry. I stayed for a week."

The lock on their pain was finally sprung and they began to really talk about the feelings they'd so carefully avoided. Their shared history once separated them; it has become their glue.

"I so enjoy the things we do together," Eleanor says enthusiastically. "Susan is so much more than my daughter; she's probably my only real friend in the world."

"I like to come here as a friend because my visits make her happier." Susan tenderly covers the seventy-nine-year-old woman's age-spotted hand with hers. "I know my mother loves me and I realize that she has been the one constant in my life. She's always been there, a rock. I watched my mother take care of her mother, and I remember her saying how hard it is to see your parents grow old. Now I know what that means. Now that we've become so close, I'm not ready for her to die."

Eleanor smiles playfully at her daughter. "I surely don't want you waiting around to visit me when I'm a sick old lady needing care. I want us to have fun now." She pauses and turns serious. "I know Susan believes that God saved her for something. No doubt it was for her daughter. But God also saved her for me."

Eleanor Blair
and her daughter,
Bonnie Blair

One of the most memorable moments at the 1994 Winter Olympics in Lillehammer, Norway, had nothing to do with sports. It occurred when millions of television viewers worldwide watched five-time gold-medalist Bonnie Blair climb off the ice after her 500-meter race and scale the packed stands to plunge into the Blair Bunch and throw her arms around . . . her mother.

The Blair Bunch, a battalion-sized group of friends and family that followed Bonnie on her amazing Olympic odyssey, had become something of a media attraction. But, for Bonnie, beaming Eleanor Blair was always the key face in the crowd. "Ever since I began racing as a kid, I'd always look for her," Bonnie says. "It's just comforting to know she's there. In Calgary, after I won my first medal, I didn't get to see my family for about two hours and that was very lonely. And in Albertville the only person I recognized was Don Johnson. He's great-looking and I got a kiss from him, but I don't know this guy. Where was my mom?

"So in Lillehammer I began to plan the whole week before how I could share this with her and not go through it by myself. After the race when the official gave me permission to crawl up into the stands, the first person I headed for was my mom. That was something really special for me."

Bonnie Blair was almost born on the ice, and her mother could have been her grandmother. Eleanor Blair was forty-four years old with five other children—the youngest nearly seven—when she discovered she was pregnant again.

The day she went into labor, her husband was scheduled to be a timer at a skating meet where two of their children were competing. They had always been a family of jocks and skating had emerged as the locus of their activity early on because they lived near the nation's largest ice rink—at the University of Illinois. All the children rose to be North American or national champions. Then came Bonnie.

"About three in the afternoon I started popping," Eleanor recalls, "and I thought I'd better go to the hospital instead of to the rink. My husband and the kids dropped me at the door and it was later announced over the microphone at the meet that there was another girl skater in the Blair family."

There were certainly times in Bonnie's youth when she wished her mother wasn't forty-five years older. "I think my mom was worn out by the time she got to me. In the beginning my sisters and brothers kind of raised me. But they soon were out of the house, away in college, and I became an only child. Sometimes I was jealous because my friends had younger mothers and they could discuss things with them that I had to discuss with my sisters.

"I didn't have a typical growing up. Like playing Monopoly or going to the movies or the zoo or doing kiddie things with my parents. But I got my attention in different ways. We never went on vacations as a family. Instead we traveled all over to skating competitions and counted that as our vacations. Skating was our bond."

Bonnie donned her first pair of skates at age two. Eleanor had to put them over her shoes "because I couldn't get them small enough. Many times when she was little she would qualify for a race and never skate the finals because she'd be napping. I figured she'd skate next week. What's the difference?" And that attitude never changed.

"My mother never, ever pushed me. Never criticized me. Never forced me," Bonnie says emphatically. "Whether I won or I lost she was very proud of me. I'd sometimes see other mothers in the stands yelling at their kids and I felt so sorry for them. I never had any of that."

"I knew she was doing the best she could," Eleanor says, "and she wanted to win more than I wanted her to win. I think competition was born in her. We were a competitive family, but never obsessed with it. Whether it was skating or seeing who could finish a puzzle faster, it was more like I'll beat you today and you'll beat me tomorrow."

Fortunately speed skating doesn't suffer from the cutthroat rivalry characteristic of the figure-skating world. And Bonnie was never interested in gliding around in pretty patterns. "I liked to race," she says. "The one time my friends made me wear figure skates I crashed a couple of times. I'm a clod. I don't have the gracefulness and I like speed.

"Whatever drive I had really came from within me. From *my* wanting to do it. But I knew my parents were always there to support and encourage me. I remember one time in Chicago—it was freezing, eighty below with the windchill. We'd trekked all the way there, spent the night in a motel, eaten in restaurants. That cost my parents money. We were skating at an outdoor rink and the wind was blowing something awful. I said I don't think I want to skate. They said, 'Okay. That's fine.' We'd spent all this money, and we just went home and they never said a word."

While Eleanor might have been somewhat over the age of the other mothers sipping coffee to keep warm in the stands, she was far from over the hill. The car keys were always in her hand, ready to chauffeur Bonnie to a meet or to practice. Sometimes they'd talk during the long drives and sometimes Bonnie would simply listen to the radio. "But," she says, "there was always a mutual understanding."

And at night there was always a sit-down, well-balanced family dinner. That was a ritual. "A lot of skaters make fun of me when we travel," Bonnie says, "because when I sit down to eat I want all my food on the plate at one time like I had at home. That's hard when you're living in these little efficiencies with two-burner stoves and you have to cook one thing first and then the other."

Wholesome and unassuming, that's Bonnie Blair. Her ego is the size of a postage stamp. She's the ultimate good sport; the girl next door who bakes chocolate chip cookies and hops out of the occasional limo to do her own laundry. And if you want to know why, you need only look at how she was raised. Her mother, at seventy-seven, still sells real estate, plays golf (using a cart that Bonnie surprised her with) and gives slide lectures on bringing up Bonnie Blair. This is a woman who faxes her daughter weekly roundups of her favorite soap operas when she's traveling abroad, but wouldn't let Bonnie leave home at seventeen to train in Europe because she thought it was more important that she finish high school. "The other skaters who went came back and she beat them anyway," Eleanor says.

True to the family form, Eleanor is more grateful than

impressed with the celebrity status that comes from being Bonnie Blair's mother. "How many mothers," she asks, "have a daughter who does wonderful things like take them to a taping of *Wheel of Fortune* or to lunch with President Ford and dinner with General Norman Schwarzkopf—in the same day?"

When Bonnie's hometown of Champaign, Illinois, wanted to name the street across from her high school after its famous Olympic graduate, Eleanor thought it was a lovely idea, but too disruptive. "All the people who lived on the street would have to change their address," she said. Instead, she suggested they choose some unnamed street in a new development.

"That's Mom's way of thinking of other people and not being selfish," Bonnie points out.

"I know my kids think I'm an old fogey and I have old-fashioned ideas," Eleanor says unabashedly.

Her rock-solid family values were the breakfast of champions for Bonnie Blair, fed to her daily. Now, knowing what's right is in Bonnie's bones. Like the decision at age thirty-two to hang up her competitive skates. "I wanted to skate as long as it was in my heart, but now it's time to get married and have a family and get on with the rest of my life," she says. "I always felt how lucky I was. How thankful to have a mom who gave me good ideals."

Their consideration toward each other is most apparent in their unplanned gestures. When they sat for this photo, Bonnie Blair, who has won more Olympic medals than any other American, was only worried that her unshaven knees would scratch her mother's face and that the weight of her legs in her mother's lap might make the aging woman uncomfortable.

"Now you know," says Eleanor sweetly, "why I'm so proud to be Bonnie Blair's mom."

Bonnie just blushes.

Petra Liljestrand and Alice Philipson and their daughter, Maya

Maya has two mommies.

"Alice is my squishy mom because she's soft," Maya says, making Alice wince. "When I'm sick or I want to be snuggled or I have a cooking question, I go to her.

"Petra is my interrogator mom. She's a medical sociologist and likes to know about everything. When I want to talk about something or if my computer doesn't work or I need help fixing a light switch or spelling 'sociology,' I go to her.

"If I want one of them in particular, I'll call them by name. But usually I just yell Mom and they both answer.

"They are really good parents. Good people. They're not crazy. They don't yell a lot or eat too much or make everything spotless. They're not overprotective. My friends think I have really cool parents—and I do. If somebody can't deal with my two moms, it's their problem. These are my parents and they love me. So get used to it. Sometimes I'm so bored talking about having two mothers. Hello, people out there. Hello. *What is the big deal!*"

It was Alice's idea to have a child. She suggested it to Petra after they'd been together four years. Back in the early 1980s, sperm banks weren't interested in dealing with two women who wanted to conceive a child, so they used the lesbian underground to find a doctor willing to assist them. A friend donated his sperm.

"We thought we were going to have a boy because donor insemination has a higher percentage of boys than girls," Alice says, "so we considered it a bonus when we got Maya. There were so few kids in the lesbian community back then and we knew that living in a woman's community it would be easier to have a girl."

"I would never have had a kid if it hadn't been for Alice," Petra says. "I

remember the first time Maya said 'Mom,' I cried—and I didn't even know which one of us she was talking to. We had some friends for dinner that night and they were all laughing at me because every time Maya said 'Mom,' I started crying."

Both Petra and Alice come up blank when asked for an example of any disapproval they've encountered. "We present ourselves to the world as a very positive thing," Petra says. "When we registered Maya for kindergarten, we both introduced ourselves as her mother. The principal looked at the birth certificate, which said 'donor insemination,' and then she looked at us and said, 'Ahh. We have a New Age kid here.' And that was that."

The response would probably have been very different had they been living in the heart of the Bible Belt instead of in Berkeley, California. But even in this liberal stronghold, Maya's moms have worked hard to make her life as normal as possible. "We chose where we live and always had a network of accepting people around. Our house has been very open," Alice says. "We moved into it before Maya started school so I could have my law practice at home and there would always be a mom around."

The two mothers fight about child rearing just like any heterosexual couple and, compared to that model, they are more stable than many marriages. "We were in a parent co-op when Maya was three," Alice says. "Of the twelve families, only two of us are still together. Most of our straight-couple friends have split."

"They've been together twenty years, you know," Maya points out. "They've been totally constant."

"We live this boring upper-middle-class lifestyle," Alice says. "We go hiking in Europe, fix the house, have company for dinner, play cards, watch *Star Trek,* share books, read a lot and talk."

Maya, a cheerful, well-adjusted fourteen-year-old, has to dig deep to find something to rebel against. "Most teenagers think their parents don't know anything, but there's not much I can say or do that my moms haven't gone through. I am hard pressed to find something to rant and rave about, except how embarrassing they are. I want them to look presentable. I tell them what to wear and they don't listen. Some of the pants Alice wears are really ugly." She rolls her eyes and sticks out her tongue to make her point.

Maya hasn't started to date yet, so her sexuality remains to be defined. "We figure she'll be straight, because nine out of ten people are," Alice says.

"But I think they want me to be gay," Maya cuts in.

"We don't mind if she's heterosexual. We have quite a few men in our life. The more important issue is that she be with somebody we get along with."

Petra adds, "We just hope she doesn't pick some creep."

Whatever Maya's future holds, she has already transformed the life of her mothers.

"Besides being an incredible daughter, she has opened up so much for us," Alice says. "We have friends who don't have kids and their life passes like a placid sort of river flowing to the sea. But because of how Maya is growing and changing, our life tumbles over rocks and goes into eddies and it's so exciting to share with her.

"I was very close to my mother and having a daughter had been very special for her. She loved our relationship and I wanted to re-create that in a way unique to me. I always knew my mother loved me, but I didn't know what it felt like for her. Now I do, because that's how I love Maya."

As for Maya, she feels twice blessed.

"I am very lucky," she says, "because my mothers are very special and I love them both very much. A lot of kids don't even like their parents. If they were different people they could easily smother me. But they know when to keep their mouths closed, so we get along great. And I have an advantage none of my friends do. Most of them have more close relationships with their moms than they do with their dads. They think it's really nice that I get to have two moms. I never feel I'm missing anything."

Darlene Davenport and her daughter, Susan Davenport

"Boo." Susan jumps from behind the door. "Did I scare you, Mom?"
Susan acts like a typical five-year-old. She plays with her doll, Nancy. She watches *Sesame Street,* where she learned to count from one to ten in Spanish. Most days she needs a little help getting dressed because she tends to dawdle. She's crazy about Barney, country music and adding new words to her vocabulary. She's just mastered "absolutely," which means for the next few weeks everything will be absolutely something.

There's just one thing wrong with this picture. Susan, with her flirty blue eyes, blond curls and cheerful smile, isn't a child. She's twenty-five years old.

At birth, Susan was the answer to every mother's prayer for a healthy baby. "I thought she was the most beautiful baby I'd ever seen," Darlene says. "I imagined her growing up, going to proms, having boyfriends, and making me a grandmother."

Then, at seven months, Susan was stricken with a deadly case of pneumonia. Her temperature shot sky-high, her breathing stopped and she had to be revived by mouth-to-mouth resuscitation. After that the epileptic seizures started, launching the family on an endless round of medications, hospitalizations, special diets and doctor-shopping in an attempt to control them.

Once Susan started walking, she had to wear a helmet because the unexpected seizures would propel her forward until she fell flat on her face. But the worst damage had occurred inside her head. A psychological test when she was three showed Susan to have the developmental age of an eighteen-month-old.

At that point, having another child was not an option for Darlene because Susan had been diagnosed with a genetic brain disorder, thought to be transmitted by one of her parents. Years later, when it was too late to start a family, that diagnosis was found to be a mistake. Eventually, Darlene's marriage dissolved, due in part to the strain of raising a child with such severe physical and emotional disabilities. Darlene has since remarried.

"Since Susan is my only child, I don't know what normal would be like," Darlene says. "Taking care of her has become a way of life for me. I could never live with myself if I put her in an institution. Besides, nobody would watch over her like I do. I'm very protective. What worries me most is what will happen after I'm gone. I was recently hospitalized myself. When the doctor told me I'd be away from home eleven days, I started to cry. Not because I had concerns about *my* health—I could live with anything—but I was worried about my responsibilities to Susan. I don't mind them, though it would be wonderful if she could understand and thank me. But she's so darn lovable that my reward comes from all the enjoyment she gives me."

Susan has never lost the sweet and affectionate playfulness of a little girl. And, like most children, she says the cutest things. "I remember years ago when I took her to the Mayo Clinic," Darlene recalls. "I was all alone and scared to death. I had to rent a car and drive two hours from the airport in a snowstorm with a child who might have a seizure at any minute. We finally got to the hotel, and we were given a room on the second floor with no elevator and we had two suitcases. I asked her to carry up her own suitcase and she said, 'No. I'm too young to work.' Another time I got a call from her teacher asking me if I'd gotten the note he'd sent home about her behavior. I asked Susan where it was and she said, 'I threw it in the garbage because it was garbage.' She just makes me laugh."

And sometimes cry. At the sheltered workshop where Susan goes every day, they pack the synthetic diamonds sold on a home shopping network. Last Christmas, Susan chose one of the rings for her mother. "Because I love her," she says. "And I wrote on the card, 'Merry Christmas and Happy New Year. Good time to you and all your friends. I love you. Me.' "

Occasionally Darlene allows herself to feel some perfectly normal disappointments. "With my friends' children going to college and getting married, I sometimes feel a tiny bit cheated. A few years ago we found my wedding dress and Susan tried it on. She looked beautiful and that's when the sadness hit me, because it's never going to happen." Darlene hastily stuffed the dress back in its box. There was no reason to preserve it.

Darlene copes by concentrating on what Susan brings to her, not what she's lost. "I am grateful for what I have: for the nights she doesn't seizure; for people who can relate to her; for my health, so I can take care of her. People take so much for granted. A sunny day. Their kids going off to school. I never know what's going to happen with Susan. She has taught me to appreciate life and every good day there is. I just accept all the love and affection she gives me and I'm happy about that."

And who takes care of Darlene?

"Nobody," she says. "I'm the mother."

Nora Cashion and her daughters, Madeline and Bridget McMahon

Nora Cashion had seen and read enough to expect her daughters' teen years to be rough and stormy. Yet nothing quite prepared her for the full-blown hurricane that wreaked havoc with the orderly landscape of her home.

"Quite frankly, the change that took place in our household was pretty abrupt," she says. "The three of us had been such a team for so long. Really ungodly close. Since my divorce, we'd built this very intimate kind of cozy connectedness. Even up to her freshman year in high school, Bridget would come into my room late at night and we'd have long chats about some topic she'd be enthusiastic about. We've always been big readers and shared novels. And then things just changed. There was no smooth transition. The girls became teenagers and that sweetness time from eight to twelve when they'd been very attached was suddenly gone."

Until then Nora had managed fairly well without a husband in her life. She'd built a successful career as a self-employed pharmaceutical products marketing consultant. She and her daughters lived in a large, tastefully decorated, book-filled brick home in a racially mixed, gentrified neighborhood. "Given the limited spectrum of opportunities for a single mother with absolutely no family around for support, I tried to give the girls what I thought was important in life," she says. "Keep a fertile mind. Enjoy what the city has to offer. Keep them on track."

There were certainly minor hints of rebellion—like when Bridget gave up the flute in ninth grade.

"Music was really important to Mom," Bridget says in her low, flat voice. "She never forced me to play the flute, but when I quit, it was a big struggle. I'd been doing it more for her than for me anyhow, and I got these little lectures about how it brought her so much joy in her life and why couldn't I do it for myself and try to realize my potential. Then my younger sister quit the piano, too."

"That was truly sad for me," Nora admits.

But it wasn't as upsetting as when the girls became vegetarians. "I was a real foodie and I'd really enjoyed preparing meals," Nora says. "I wasn't trained to cook as a vegetarian. It wasn't simply that the girls became pro-vegetables. They were anti everything else, and I worried about protein. At least Bridget ate eggs; but Madeline would only eat beans. You can only eat beans so many nights in a row."

"Mom was worried about our nutrition," Bridget says sympathetically.

But she was even more worried about their souls. "Church was a sore topic," Bridget says. "I have a lot of resentment toward my parents for baptizing me and forcing me to go to Catholic school until I was fourteen. Mom thinks her religion is the right one, and it's sad, because I don't believe in it. And she should have respect for that. She made us go to church every Sunday. Madeline and I acted very rude. We'd try to sleep in, slam the car doors, refuse communion."

The tension escalated when Bridget reached high school. Her straight-A record got her admitted to a public high school designated for gifted students; yet once there, she thumbed her nose at the notion of academic achievement.

"I didn't think it was important to get good grades and work for A's. Like I was interested in writing essays and what not, but as far as tests and stuff, I didn't care," she says. "I just didn't care about, you know, getting perfect grades to go to the perfect college and live the typical mainstream life. I didn't value that and my mom was, like, why aren't you trying to get the best grades you can?"

Nora responds carefully. "I just didn't want her throwing away good grades and shutting off her future options. In those days I used to joke that the girls were in their boomerang toddler phase. They keep you up late at night. They don't communicate well. They say 'no' a lot. It was just like having a two- or three-year-old again."

Bridget's attitude toward school pretty much reflected her I-don't-care view in general. "I don't have a whole lot to be optimistic about," she says. She didn't have many close friends, and when she found one in her new school, the girl happened to be a punk. "I started listening to punk music, hanging out with punks and then dressing like them. In that scene parents are just not talked about. I wanted nothing to do with Mom. You know, like everyone wants to shock their parents. So I dyed my hair red, then canary green. It's been pink, orange, purple, black. Sometimes more than one color at once."

"She had long, rich, thick hair you could die for," Nora says wistfully. When Bridget grimaces, she adds, "Sorry, honey, but a mom is allowed to say those things. Her hairstyle was outrageous, but it was superficial. It just didn't faze me that much. You're supposed to pick your battles and this wasn't one of them. I set rules in the house, but I didn't draw lines in the sand."

For Nora, the worst of times was when they stopped communicating. The year or so after Bridget got heavily into punk, they barely spoke, except to battle over Bridget's boyfriend, her underage drinking and her blatant irresponsibility. "I'm not a very responsible person," Bridget acknowledges. "I was always late or I didn't show up at all. I'd end up spending the night at a friend's house and didn't call to say where I was."

Nora, who describes herself as "analytical by nature," dealt with her daughter's infuriating behavior primarily by trying to understand her. "Mostly I was confused," she says. "I couldn't figure out what the hell was happening to my child. Okay, Bridget's decided the traditional route is not for her. Then where is she heading? And is she staying enough on track that she isn't going to compromise herself? Also I was worried about her safety."

"I cared that she was upset, but I cared more about hanging out and having fun," Bridget says. "I was testing my limits. This rebellion thing is more against society than against my mom. She's so tolerant, like unless I became an ax murderer or something, I feel secure I will always have a home base."

Things began to improve when Bridget finally moved out and started college. But she dropped out after one semester. Nora could accept that Bridget needed time to find herself; however, she insisted her daughter do *something*.

Punk kids with high school educations aren't terribly employable—even a smart one like Bridget, whose favorite book is *The Stranger* by existentialist novelist Albert Camus. She reluctantly ended up relocating to upstate Pennsylvania when her father finally hired her at his commercial bakery, where she packs bread into cartons. Their relationship is strained; he's far more rigid and conservative than his ex-wife. Most weekends Bridget takes a three-hour bus ride back to her mother's house in Philadelphia.

Despite their obvious differences, Nora welcomes Bridget's company. "I try to think about Bridget's long-term best interest," Nora says. "I actually empathize with her more than she realizes. I understand the struggles of being nineteen, wanting to be your own person, not knowing what you want to do."

Nora admits that her tolerance has been partly motivated by her fear of losing Bridget. "I certainly have asked myself: Was I a good enough mother?" Nora says. "You read all the time where families are estranged. I can't think of a more horrible prospect. If Bridget looks at the world in unconventional ways, she could very well throw out all conventional assumptions and become a stranger to me."

But that seems unlikely.

"I really respect my mom and I listen to her now about a lot of things because I realize she was right," Bridget says. "She thinks I think she doesn't know anything and I don't value what she says, but I do. Like I definitely can't see myself in twenty years sporting a Mohawk and wearing tons of metal. Even though I dress like this, I'm thinking of going to fashion school, like fashion buying or design. But I won't be working in some dumb mainstream job where I'm just collecting money, with two kids and two cars in the garage, going to church every Sunday and voting for whatever Republican candidate comes along. So I think it's stupid for somebody to look at me and think I had bad parents. Because I didn't turn out bad. I turned out good."

"Yes, honey, you have. You are a good girl," Nora says, and it's obvious that she means it. "In some ways Bridget has brought me up short and made me realize that a daughter is not some puppet of yours that you are going to turn into a perfect little model to show off. She is a real live human being, moving into adulthood, who has to be treated as an individual. You would never presume to control another adult, and for a person like me who likes to control, that has been a very important lesson.

"There is a bittersweet quality to all of this. We are never going to live the way we did when she was young and we had a special closeness with a lot of cozy parts. That has to change. I have some sadness about that. But it has to be."

Bridget has been listening to her mother intently. "My dad wants me to live my life his way," she says. "But I know now that my mom just wants me to be happy."

Lila Bishop and her daughter, Tara Bishop

Lila and Tara have camped in tents in remote Bhutan, traveled on the dusty roads of India and trekked through the mountains of Nepal. But their most difficult journey has been navigating the uncharted path from my mother/myself to my mother/my friend.

"I think the work of a daughter, especially in her twenties," Tara says, "is negotiating how to separate from her mother and find that line between being close with her and still being your own person. How do you establish that middle ground where you can become an adult and an individual with your own life while at the same time hold on to this very deep connection you had as a child?"

It certainly helps if you have a mother like Lila, who's willing to be a partner.

"Over thirty-one years Tara and I have always been fairly open and communicated in a very easy way," Lila says. "I think as a parent I probably confided in her more than I should have, but she always seemed to understand. It's like this dance we do where we both know the steps."

Their reliance on each other took root early on. When Tara was four, her parents carted her and her brother off to Nepal, where her father worked on his doctoral thesis in cultural geography. For eighteen months they lived in a four-person tent and traversed the mountainous nation, a little unit unto themselves. Coming home to the civilized world of Bethesda, Maryland, was especially difficult for Tara. "I immediately went into a private school with all these kids who were very bright," she says, "and it was like I was from a different planet. It took me years to get into the social groove because we didn't have a television."

It wasn't until Tara left her teens that a crisis involving a relationship created the first real breach between her and Lila. "I had to take a stand," Tara says, "that I was going to do this, even though it may not be in accord with what Mom wanted."

"And I had to make the conscious decision," says Lila, "that while I thought this person was wrong for Tara, I would find a way to accept this because I wasn't going to lose my daughter. But it definitely interfered with our old pattern of communication."

After four uneasy years, that relationship ended. The next crisis Tara and Lila faced brought them to a new plateau. In 1994, Tara's father, Barry, died in a car accident; Lila survived.

"Dad's death underscored that no matter how close Mom and I are, we're very different and had very different ways of experiencing that loss," Tara says with a level of insight one might expect from a young woman with a doctorate in psychology. "Somehow that understanding freed me to grow up and recognize I could be an individualized adult and still have this great, warm relationship with my mom. I can't say what it was that shifted, but I finally feel comfortable being separate from her, when at earlier times I was really scared of what would happen if I stood on my own and did my own thing. Now I know that I can claim my own life and we can still be extremely connected. Mom makes me sparkle. I feel incredibly seen and loved by her. When I'm with her, I feel genuinely who I am."

"You just made me feel terrific, Tara," her mother says as they sit with their arms cozily draped around one another. "That's exactly what I'd want to hear from somebody I love. You reconfirm who I am. I feel good about myself when I've been with you. Your approval has more weight to it because you're my daughter."

Lila has discovered what often comes as a surprise to mothers: their daughters can be wonderful teachers, too. "I love the way Tara looks at life. By her example, she has taught me about independence. I married at twenty and was afraid to do so many things that I'm just coming around to at age sixty."

"Well, you supported my independence because you were trying to figure out how to do it for yourself," Tara counters, underscoring that what they admire in each other frequently mirrors what they value in themselves.

The test of how successfully they'd redesigned their adult relationship became apparent at the end of an emotionally taxing mission. Barry Bishop had been part of the first American expedition to conquer Mount Everest and he'd told Lila that he wanted to be cremated and have his ashes dispersed among those majestic mountains. Lila had been leading treks to Nepal for many summers when she was on vacation from her teaching job, so it was easy to honor his request. To have Tara join her was a bonus.

For two months they traveled, a mother and daughter honoring their husband and father by scattering his remains at the places he loved. They held hands as monks chanted from the Tibetan Book of the Dead and huddled together in their tent, giggling as they shared memories. "We hang out extremely well together," Tara says. "This trip really helped create a respect around our boundaries. Mom truly started to see me as an adult."

Tara returned to the States first; Lila stayed abroad. "Two weeks after Tara left me in Katmandu," Lila says, "I got a phone call saying she was married to someone who hadn't even been in her life before she got home. To tell you the truth, I was stunned and shocked and, frankly, a bit appalled. But I was as sure as I'd been years before that I wasn't going to lose Tara."

"I knew I'd met my soul mate," Tara says, explaining her rash behavior. "But just as important, I felt I could make a decision like getting married without my mother being here, and she would rise to the occasion. I'll admit I was anxious for a minute after the phone call, and then she wrote me this fabulous letter."

Dear Tara, it began.

. . . I can't even imagine all the components that came together in your decision but you are trusting your feelings and so I must do the same. . . . Passion doesn't always give one 20/20 vision and this is my greatest concern for you. . . . We all lost one person suddenly to a September day. Perhaps this new person in our lives will be a gift for us all. . . . I can look at this many ways and I have decided that my heart will be open to you both. . . . Take good care of yourself, Mrs. Mortensen. May your joy and your love continue.

Love . . . Mom

Edna Austin and
her daughter, Patti Austin

So, Patti, what's the best piece of advice your mother ever gave you?

"Oh, that's easy. Her classic line is never hit a cripple or screw a fool."

"And you," Edna rebounds with a smirk, "never listened!"

Welcome to Mother Knows Best, starring the irreverent comedy team of Edna and Patti Austin. Cue up the theme music—the Patti Austin/James Ingram megahit "How Do You Keep the Music Playing?"—and cancel the canned laugh track. The way these two crack each other up, there's no need for outside help. Patti animatedly sets up the story; Edna deadpans a "tell it like it is" retort and they both fall apart laughing.

Patti Austin got her lessons in living from her mother and her musical education from her father. A trombonist in the Big Band era, he began training his baby to sing before she could talk by playing notes on his horn and having her repeat them vocally. Patti made her first public appearance at age four when her godmother, Dinah Washington, plunked her down on the stage of the Apollo Theater in Harlem, where she belted out "Teach Me Tonight." Edna missed most of her daughter's debut. "I was in the bathroom," she says. "My kidneys float as soon as I get excited."

That meant she didn't see pint-size Patti bring down the house for chiding the band that they were playing her song in the wrong key. The precocious tot particularly impressed an up-and-coming entertainer standing in the wings. Sammy Davis, Jr., signed Patti to be part of his act, launching her career as a child performer.

Edna always made damn sure that if Patti was going to have a career, she was also going to have a normal childhood. They could traipse into Manhattan for her daughter to cut a record or appear on television in *Star Time,* but during the week Patti would attend public school and do chores like any other kid.

"One day I said to Patti when she was around five, 'Get a pail and rag and clean out the toilets,' " Edna remembers. "My husband got very indignant: 'What are you doing? All those germs in there!' I told him, 'See these two hands, buddy? They do it and she's no better than me.' I'm a firm believer that if you bring your children up to think they are like God, they believe you. Then when they get older and act like God, you penalize them. If they're demanding $125 sneakers, it's 'cause you brought them up like that. What we used to do in our house is rotate weeks where you could ask for what you wanted."

"We'd go to a store," Patti explains, "and I'd say, 'Mom, can I have that? And she'd say, 'No. It's Dad's week.' That's how I learned you don't expect everything to come to you the moment you want it, and when it doesn't, you are able to deal with it."

With Edna there was never a shortage of lessons. "When Patti was six or seven she wrote me a letter in lipstick. 'I HATE MOM.' I told her, 'Go right ahead. You can hate me. You're entitled to your opinion. I might hate you, too.' "

"I was very teed off that there was a potential for her to hate me," Patti says, laughing. "It was a real revelation. Made me realize that it was okay for me not to love her every second of the day, and it was also okay if she didn't love me every second of the day."

"Well, your children wish to God you'd love them a little bit less and like them a little bit more," Edna declares.

By the time Patti entered show business, her father had already put down his horn and both her parents were working as attendants in a state mental hospital. "We did split shifts 'cause I don't believe in babysitters," Edna says. "Nobody is gonna raise my baby like I want her to be raised. So he worked nights and I worked days."

"My parents were so bloody creative in their poverty," Patti says, "that I didn't realize how poor we were, even though we had to borrow a car to go into Manhattan two or three times a week. Not long ago I said to Mom how it was so cool the way we'd go into Central Park for a picnic after rehearsals. Those were such wonderful times and I love picnics because of them. She said,

'Honey, we had picnics because we could not afford a restaurant.' I was completely blown away."

In their family, Patti's father played the role of stage mother. "We had to ground his butt," Patti says, "because he was always like 'Wow, look at my kid!' My mother was the anchor, telling him, 'Would you please relax and calm down.' She was definitely a combination of tough love and compassion. I never heard her say, 'Wait till your father gets home.' It was the other way around."

"I would never holler," Edna interjects in the tag-team style they use to play off one another. "I would make eye contact with Patti and tell her once and only, 'Are you listening?' One of my rules was yes means yes and no means no. I have a very low tolerance for kids begging, please, Mommy, please."

"Begging would get you killed in my house," Patti picks up. "That's a very black thing, though. I grew up in Bay Shore, Long Island, when it was like farm country. There were very few black folks, except for sharecroppers who came in the summer. Most of my friends were WASPs or intellectual Jews. They would want me to do something and I'd say, 'I have to ask my mother.' Sometimes, not often, she'd say no. I'd phone Suzie or whoever and tell her my mom said no.

" 'Well,' Suzie would say, 'ask her why.'

" 'Whoa. You don't understand,' I'd answer. 'You don't ask a black mother *why*. It's like an ethnic rule.' But it was a great rule because I always knew what the boundaries were. I think Mom did a brilliant job of parenting. She made me very self-reliant in a loving way."

Curfews, for example, were never an issue. "Mom believed in self-motivation. You could stay out until three if you wanted to but you still had to get up at six o'clock."

Boyfriends weren't a problem either.

"You know how most parents are?" Edna rolls into another riff. "If you have a son, you don't mind if fifteen women are calling him. Look how popular my boy is! If you have a daughter,

come the first phone call, you're asking, 'Who is that idiot? He didn't say good evening; he has no manners.' I never had to worry about stuff like boyfriends, makeup or short clothes with Patti. She was so wrapped up in show business that if a fellow liked her, she was usually too busy. And when she had boyfriends I didn't like, I never barred them from the house. My theory was invite them over. I want to look 'em in the eye and learn to love 'em."

"To her credit she never, ever asked me why don't I get married or where are my grandchildren," Patti says. "And she'd never say a word to me about a boyfriend until it was all over. Then she'd let loose. What an idiot he was!"

"Hey." Edna shrugs. "You wouldn't have heard me anyway. It's your life. And you could easily turn around and say to me, 'The guy you picked isn't so hot either.'"

When Patti was fifteen years old, Edna developed a very serious case of cancer of the cervix that was treated with a radical new radiation insert procedure. "Mom glowed for a while and she still vibrates a little," Patti jokes. "That's why we call her the original hot mama." Then she turns serious.

"I went from an A to a D average overnight in school. I could not talk about what was going on. I was terrified she was going to die, and how would I deal with it? What will I do? My mother is my life!!! She was just so amazing. She's always had this high level of matter-of-factness about things. This is what it is with no rose-colored glasses. She insisted I go out to California for the summer to stay with my godfather, Quincy Jones.

"I didn't want to leave, and she said, 'You must go. I don't want you to stand around and watch me dying, if I'm dying, or living, if I'm living. Either I'll be fine or I won't. And if I die I'll be with you every day. Besides, there's no way you're getting rid of me.'"

"Most people I came in contact in the hospital," Edna interrupts, "were groaning, 'Oh, why me? Oh, why me?' And I always said, 'Why not me?' Who's got it easy? If you are breathing, you have it hard."

"That's our big joke now whenever anything happens to us," Patti says. "We look at each other and go, 'Why me! Why me!' Because it's like 'Why not you? Who the hell are you?' What I learned from the way my mother went through her cancer is that it's very important when things become horrible to become phenomenally positive. I really believe in things spiritual, and if you feel negative inside yourself, that's what the universe gives back to you. My mother's whole life is manifested positive thinking."

"Life is a joke." Edna gets the last word. "When you lose your humor, you lose your life."

*Marjorie Margolies
Mezvinsky and
her daughters,
Holly Mezvinsky
and Lee Heh Margolies*

arjorie Mezvinsky can still recall in perfect detail the first time she met her daughter Lee Heh. "It was twenty-six years ago in a little three-story stucco house in an orphanage in Korea. I was handed a file of a little six-year-old girl, so little, with bone-straight hair. They kept saying she was number one, meaning, I think, that she was the top child in the orphanage. I'd asked for a girl because I thought it would be easier than a boy, not knowing if there would ever be a father in the picture. And then this pint-size person walked in and said, 'How do you do.' That was all she knew in English. I didn't hug her, because I didn't know if it was the right thing to do, but I was just overwhelmed with feelings. How did it happen that *she* was chosen for *me?* We went out for ice cream and she wanted chocolate. I thought that was the first thing I knew about her. She liked chocolate."

Back in 1970, before Murphy Brown shredded the stigma of single motherhood for professional women, the idea that a real, unmarried, twenty-six-year-old television reporter would adopt a child was radical in the extreme. Marjorie had done a series on hard-to-place kids for her television news program and "it seemed foolish to wait," she says. "I had the means, the energy and the passion. I loved children, and I cared less about getting married and more about being a parent. It seemed a good thing to adopt a kid who would otherwise not have a home. And I felt it was the ultimate kind of selfishness to need a child who had my looks and my genes. My parents thought I was crazy. But they said, 'You've never done anything we were ashamed of,' and they gave me total support."

Lee Heh arrived in America on the youngest student visa ever issued; it was the quickest way to get her into the country. The first thing her new mother did was to chop off her own waist-length dark hair to her shoulders to match her daughter's. "I thought people could say, 'Oh, you look like your mother. You both have long hair.' "

Years later it would sometimes bother Lee Heh when kids pointed out that her mom didn't look at all like her. But other than appearances, they turned out to be beautifully matched. Lee Heh was an ideal choice for a single mother: a very bright, well-behaved child, already tuned to being a people-pleaser. "She liked apples," Marjorie remembers. "The first night in my apartment, we only had one apple and she made my mother cut it in four pieces to share with everyone." From the start, Lee Heh desperately wanted to be accepted. "We went skiing about a year after she came," Marjorie says, "and she fell and broke her ankle. The first thing Lee Heh said in her broken English was 'Are you going to send me back? In Korea they told me if I wasn't good I'd be sent back.' "

Today, thirty-two-year-old Lee Heh explains, "I was motivated to do well because I wanted to be good, to be liked and to make sure I did things right."

"And I was just the opposite," says her twenty-eight-year-old Vietnamese sister, Holly. "I apparently arrived, picked up a cigarette and started smoking. I had the attitude that it's my world, and if Mom likes me, great! If not, beat it!"

Holly joined the family four years after Lee Heh. "I think it's very tough to be an only child and it was just so easy the first time," Marjorie says, explaining her decision to adopt a second daughter. "I already had all these outgrown clothes from Lee Heh anyway. So I got the *Today* show to send me on an assignment to Vietnam, and I found Holly."

"I remember Mom asking me if I would be interested in having a sister," Lee Heh recalls. "And I said, 'No!' "

It wasn't at all like she promised. "Holly was a definite challenge," Marjorie admits in a classic understatement about the tornado who swept into their harmonious home. Normal behavior for Holly was a kicking and screaming tantrum. She peppered her talk with American swear words, learned from spending the first six years of her life in the postwar streets. When she wanted something, she simply took it. "There were many days," Marjorie says, "when I'd lie down at night and say to myself: God, why have I done this? But I could always see Holly was going to be fabulous. Here is this kid who's alive because she's a survivor. She was feisty and loving and very funny. Under no circumstances would I give up on her."

Marjorie has a way of forgetting those supremely difficult years. "The fabric of my personality is let's figure out how we can make this work, as opposed to settling on things that don't work. So I tend not to recollect the negatives."

"My mother is a Pollyanna," Lee Heh says gently. "She has this great 'it's not a big deal' life attitude."

When her daughters were fourteen and ten, Marjorie unexpectedly found them a father. She interviewed then Congressman Ed Mezvinsky, and it was love at first question.

Marjorie remembers sitting on the couch saying to Lee Heh, "Sweetie, we're going to get married." The teenager was not happy. "Your credibility is not so hot, Mom. The last time you told me you were going to bring someone into the house that I would enjoy it was Holly!"

"My mother has a very good way of selling an idea," Lee Heh explains. The next sales pitch was her pregnancy. To Ed's four daughters by a previous marriage were added two sons from their union and later on a couple of Vietnamese refugee boys who somehow joined the family. While mothering this passel of kids, Marjorie maintained an active television career, commuting between her job in Washington and her home in Philadelphia. She wrote two books and got elected to the U.S. House of Representatives for one term. As it turned out, her whirlwind professional life created more conflicts for her daughters than what might have developed from their racial, ethnic or adoptive issues.

"I'm American and I'm Jewish," Holly says flat out. "That's how I was raised and I'm proud of it. But my mom told me a long time ago, point-blank, 'You kids are the most important things to me, but you're not the only thing. My career is also very important.' For a long time that gave me a perfect excuse for my failures. I could say: It was my mother. She wasn't there for me. But I'm very much past that now."

Lee Heh, who also works in television, as a producer, often suffers from comparisons with her mother. "I hear, 'Oh, you're like your mom; you're in TV.' Or 'Aren't you Marjorie Margolies' daughter?' It's really annoying. Sometimes I wonder if I'm ever going to shake her off. At the same time I respect my mom for doing more with her life than sitting home raising kids. You have to give up a lot to achieve what she has achieved. She did a lot of apologizing to us about being away from home, and I feel bad about that. She wasn't exactly playing around at Elizabeth Arden. She was working her butt off. Her mantra was always about quality versus quantity time. But looking back, I could have used a little more of the quantity."

"Well, Dad's never here," Holly points out. "And no one complains about that. Certainly I wouldn't be who I am if it wasn't for Mom. I'm a very different person from when I got off that plane."

Lee Heh agrees. "Mom *is* an incredible parent. There are very few people as good as she is. She has this optimistic view that things are going to work out no matter what. Like with us. We'll be okay because she loves us and we're her daughters."

"Well, gosh, thank you," Marjorie says, almost surprised. "It's true I do think attitude is everything."

But there is one thing that even her positive outlook can't change: the distance between her daughters. Her great disappointment is that her girls have never really connected with each other.

"It's not that we fight," Lee Heh explains. "We just don't relate. It's more like our sister bond has been nonexistent."

That has forced Marjorie to develop strong, yet quite separate relationships with each of her daughters.

"I love them both, and I see good things in both of them," she says. "But you are dealt the hand you get and you work with it as best you can. I understood early on that they were very different children who were going to go their own ways. Fortunately they've had many other siblings to be close to. I absolutely know they would like each other if they would only give themselves the chance."

"Oh God, here we go," Lee Heh says. "It's not like you haven't made attempts."

"You know what I mean," Marjorie answers patiently. "If somebody asked me if there was one thing in my life that I could fix, that would be Lee Heh and Holly. But it's one thing I can't control. Maybe my daughters will be like my sister and me. We didn't have much in common when we were growing up and we've just recently begun connecting as adults. That's why I still have hope."

Of course she does. She's their mother!

Anna Davis and
her daughter, Diana Garrett

When a woman gives birth to a daughter, something in the deep
recesses of her mind, where hopes lie unexpressed, breathes a sigh of
relief. "Now I will have someone to take care of me in my old age."
Diana Garrett had never planned to bring her mother into her home. "Mother
always said she never wanted to be a burden to her children and that we should
put her in a nursing home. But I found out later she did not mean that. When
she became more or less disabled, she'd say, 'Well, I can come live with you,' and I
used to tell her that we couldn't make it together. She is very strong-willed and
controlling. When she fell and broke her collarbone in 1988, I brought her to my
house, and she drove me crazy. When I'd go out she'd be at the window
watching, and when I came back she'd be at the window waiting."

Anna recovered sufficiently from that accident to return to her own home—
but not for long. She started to become forgetful—and she knew it. She'd
complain endlessly to Diana, "This memory of mine. This memory of mine."

At eighty-nine Anna was still living alone, but barely making it, despite daily
visits from Diana. "It really saddened me," Diana says, sitting in the living room of
her spotless row house amid her vast collection of house plants. "Mother had been
very independent since my father died in 1963. But I could see her going
downhill. I had to nail the windows open in her apartment so she could get some
air because she'd shut them and turn off the fan when I left. Then one really hot
day I found her sitting on the commode in the dining room, just out of it and
suffering something awful from the heat. I took her to the hospital, and when she
was ready to be discharged I just decided all of a sudden to bring her here. My
sister had upped and died on me in an automobile accident and my brothers, well,
you know how it is. So all this is on me."

Diana still considered the possibility of a nursing home until she put her mother
into what she thought was a very good one while she took a week's vacation. On
her return she found Anna sitting in dirty clothes, soiled with her own feces. "Her

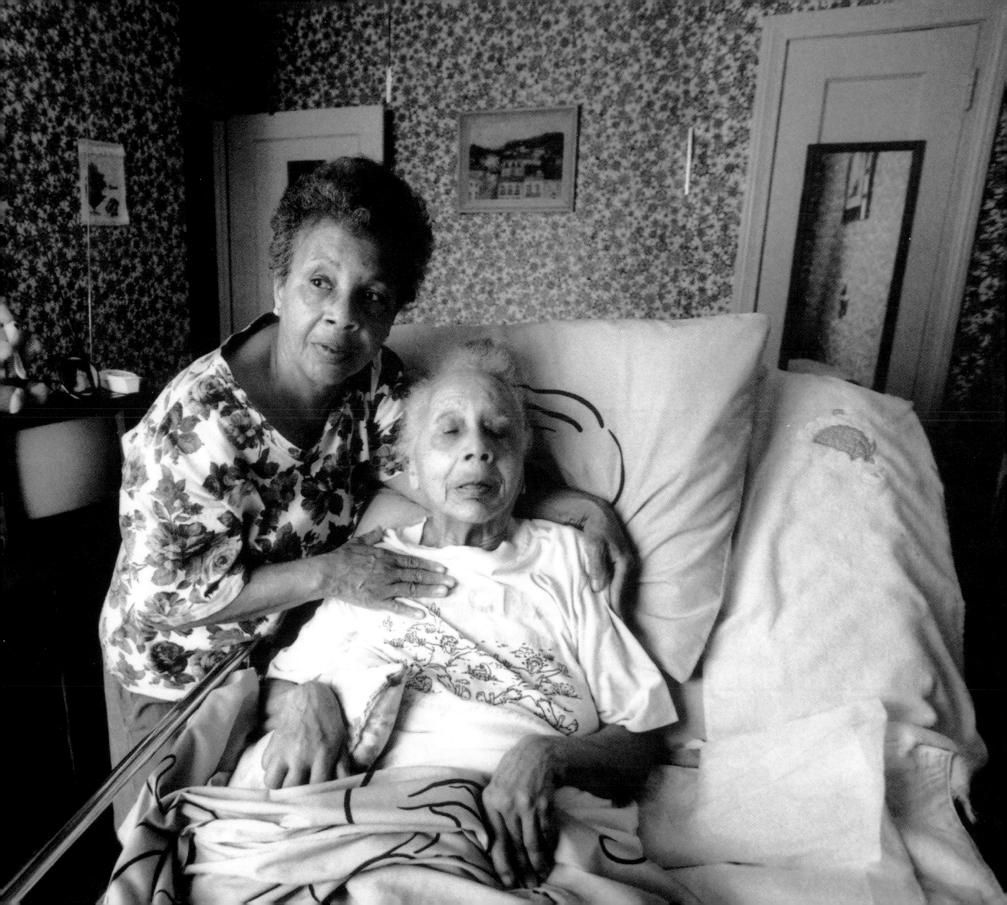

feet were swollen. She smelled. There was no hot water. No diapers. That's what made me decide she had to live with me."

In 1994 Anna suddenly stopped walking. The doctors thought she'd had an undiagnosed stroke. "Then she just stopped talking, too. The only thing she'd say was 'Oh, boy. Oh, boy.' If anything upset her, 'Oh, boy. Oh, boy.' "

Gradually even that reaction slipped away. Today Anna spends her life curled in a lounge chair in a sterile bedroom with black-and-white-patterned wallpaper. The radio is tuned to church music; the TV is usually off. Her childlike body sits motionless, her reed-thin arms and legs, useless. Yet she looks ready to go visiting. Her once-flaming red hair is perfectly done in a snow-white topknot and her unlined face is blazoned by a lipsticked mouth.

Except for the homemaker who comes in an hour a day, Diana, a retired sixty-seven-year-old civil servant, is the sole caretaker for her invalid ninety-two-year-old mother. She feeds her soupy food that doesn't need to be chewed, bathes her, changes her diapers, suctions the phlegm from her congested chest and talks to her much the way a young mother chatters to a baby. "I believe she knows what I'm saying. I ask her: Do you want such and such? If you understand, blink your eyes. And she does."

Diana harbors no resentment for the limitations her caretaker role places on her life. "I'd probably take more vacations if she weren't here but I've never been one to go much. I'm not a social butterfly and I've always been low-keyed." Her main outings are church on Sunday and charity work on Wednesdays, when she delivers meals-on-wheels for an AIDS organization.

"I just couldn't put my mother in a nursing home. She was a tough old woman, but I will never forget the nice things she did for me when my three sons and I lived with her for seven years. I was twenty-two. My husband had left us and she took care of everything until I got a job and then babysat while I worked. That's when we became close. In later years we took trips together. She looked upon me as a buddy, a friend.

"I don't feel I'm obligated to take care of her just because she's my mother. In fact, I get really upset when people feel sorry for my lifestyle. 'Oh, you have such a burden. You can't go here or there.' I don't look at it that way. I'm doing what's right, not what's expected of me. My mother took care of me because mothers are supposed to take care of their children. I take care of her because I want to. You know what frightens me? I worry that she'll live to be a hundred and I'll be old and not able to care for both of us."

It is 8 P.M., the end of a typical day for Diana and her mother. Diana's monotonous daily routine begins at 7:30 with her bath and coffee, after which she gives her mother her medications, exercises her legs and arms and sponges her down. "Even though the health-care worker bathes her, I don't want her to find her dirty in case she's had a little accident." After lunch Diana will leave her mother alone for an hour or two to run to the market or the post office. "I can't be here every minute and I know she can't get out of her chair. I just have to depend on the good Lord to take care of her."

At 4 P.M. she feeds her mother dinner and moves her inert body from the chair to the bed using a mechanical lift. By then it's time for Diana to eat and relax a bit until she changes her mother's diaper and beds her down for the night.

"It's time to say our prayers, Mother."

Anna blinks.

"Thank you, Lord, for all you've done for us. Please keep us safe through the night. Bless us, our church, our minister and our families. Amen."

Anna blinks.

Diana opens the Bible. "What psalm shall we read tonight? How about number three?"

Anna blinks.

When Diana finishes the psalm, she picks up a little bottle of perfume from the bureau and dabs a touch on her mother's neck. "This is for sweet dreams." She gently kisses her mother's smooth, ancient cheek. "Have a pleasant sleep, Mother, and sweet dreams."

Anna blinks twice.

Lynn Redgrave
and her daughters,
Kelly and Annabel Redgrave Clark

Lynn Redgrave is a woman of many grand achievements: Oscar-winning movie actress, writer, Broadway and television star. But she'd like to be remembered as the mother who sued Universal Pictures for not being allowed to breast-feed her baby daughter on the job.

The landmark lawsuit dates back to the early 1980s—long before anybody had thought of Take Your Daughter to Work Day—when Lynn was starring in a TV series called *House Calls*.

"My makeup call was around six-thirty in the morning and we usually got through at seven at night," she begins her story. "I don't think any mother and baby should be separated for that many hours a day. So there was no question I would take Annabel with me, because how else was I going to nurse her? Anyway, there was a series of discussions with the studio when she was two weeks old, and they said I couldn't bring the baby to work because it would be too disruptive, etc. Which was ridiculous. I'd had two children before [a son and a daughter]. I wouldn't hold anybody up. I'd be off quietly in my trailer. But they said no, I couldn't come with her. And my husband, John, told them, 'Then she can't come at all.'

"I have never felt such distress. I loved being pregnant. I loved having children and nursing them and being with them. At a time when I should have felt the utmost joy, suddenly my job in a hit show was gone and I ended up dragging Annabel around to talk shows to hold forth on all this."

In the ensuing furor, NOW and the La Leche League rallied to Lynn's defense, causing Universal initially to back down. "They said I'd been outrageous. Of course they welcomed me and my baby. I was simply being an unscrupulous actress trying to up my fee. But I became the butt of jokes on Johnny Carson's monologue about breast-feeding Ed McMahon and it tasting like whiskey. It got

really gross. People would come up to us in the supermarket and ask, 'Is this the famous baby? The one you wanted to breast-feed?' So we sued for wrongful dismissal and sex discrimination on the basis that nobody asked a male actor what he did in the privacy of his dressing room, so long as he showed up and did his job."

Taking a stand for motherhood had a higher price than Lynn ever imagined. For a time she was professionally banished to an official "don't hire" list. The issue became a personal obsession. "This really opened my eyes to the plight of working mothers," Lynn says. "I started speaking publicly on their behalf. I testified before a Senate committee on day care." Unfortunately, after fifteen years of legal wrangling, they lost the case. "But in a way we didn't," Lynn points out. "Eventually all the studios built day care. I'm very proud that in a small way this controversy made a difference for other people."

Lynn Redgrave's commitment to a very involved parenting style developed out of what she'd missed growing up. "My mum was absolutely adorable to me. We were very, very close for many years. I was her favorite and my role was to be the one who kept everybody amused. But she was never the hands-on mum I think I have been to my daughters."

As the children of a famous and successful acting family, Lynn and her sister, Vanessa, were cared for by nannies, who took them to the theater to see their parents at work. "There was an adult world and a child world. Mother would visit us in the nursery or we'd be dressed up to go downstairs to visit them," Lynn reminisces. "But we were kept very separate. So I wanted to have the inclusive sort of family life that I hadn't had as a child. I wanted my kids to be very much a part of everything."

Her girls will tell that's exactly how they felt, even though their mother's demanding career often took her away from home—a delightfully untidy old place high up in a rugged canyon near Los Angeles that the family shares with dogs, cats and horses. There is stuff everywhere—posters, photos, old toys, a cushy red sofa, a wicker chair, a TV with a giant screen, plants crying for water. Nothing in the house matches, but everything seems to have some personal meaning.

"My memories of Mom growing up are not many, because she was often working. But all of them are great," says Kelly, who is eleven years older than her sister Annabel. "When Mom was with us, she went out of her way to make a really comfy home. Very down-to-earth. You would imagine someone in that position would be pushy and go overboard just trying to do too much or entertain you, but she never did that. We had wonderful evenings at home. Mom is an amazing cook. She just knows how, in a very simple way, to make a little situation into an occasion."

When Kelly was little and Lynn needed to go off to do a play in Colorado or Chicago, she often took her daughter on the road with her. "We'd do special things," Kelly recalls. "Have mommy/daughter days. I remember being away with Mom and having all my Barbie dolls with me. I loved Barbies. She would sit down and say, 'Okay. We're going to play Barbies for an hour,' and she would help make up stories with me or sew dresses from some incredible fabric she'd got from the costume department of the show she was in.

"I never felt Mom wasn't available. Even on the end of the phone, you could always go into great detail, so the connection was never broken. When I was seventeen or something and lost my virginity, she was away in New York and all she wanted to know over the phone was: Did he wear his galoshes?"

Kelly and Lynn are proof that when a mother understands her daughter's need for growing space, they can survive a time apart and come back together even closer. From age seventeen to twenty-one, Kelly left America and moved to England where she lived for a while with her aunt Vanessa and studied drama.

"I always felt Kelly was looking for her place in the world," Lynn explains. "She was in a great deal of turmoil and I was sad to have her so far away, but I thought it would be the making of her. To a certain extent, it was. Then she moved back to New York and lived with me for nine months. We were like roommates. It was wonderful. We had our little rituals, like tea in the afternoon, or when I got home from the theater, we'd have great talks. And on Monday nights, when I didn't work, we'd watch trashy television."

Frank. Open. Accepting. And fun. That is the hallmark of Lynn's interactions with her daughters, whether it's a conversation about sex or a shopping spree. Annabel, for instance, gets no objections from her mother for her insistence on wearing nothing but vintage clothing.

"I have a friend whose mother won't let her buy secondhand clothes," Annabel exclaims. "She says it's immoral! But I couldn't imagine my mother being like that. I have a really good relationship with her compared to a lot of kids. I have so much respect for her. We can talk about anything. Like she really understands that I have my own style."

"Of course you do, dear," Lynn easily agrees. "I want you to express yourself. It's a way of finding who you are."

For Lynn Redgrave the essence of being a good mother is letting her daughters seek their own path—and giving them guidance *if* they ask for it. When Kelly mentioned one day at breakfast that she was exploring a relationship with another woman, Lynn's reaction was a sanguine "That's nice, dear. Would you like more tea?"

"I tried to be real cool about it," Lynn reasons. "Because my father was bisexual, I wasn't exactly shocked. I didn't go, 'Oh my god!' I probably saw it in Kelly before she did. The bottom line is I only want her—and Annabel as well—to be fulfilled and happy. In their work. In their personal life. In everything. Annabel already has a great sense of herself, and when Kelly brought this up, I had a wonderful feeling of relief that maybe this would be a way for Kelly to finally find Kelly. In finding yourself you become freer. All I want for my daughters is for them to be as free as I became."

Irene Rawlings and her daughter, Liz Rawlings

Irene Rawlings, a short, stocky, popular Denver talk-show host and journalist, has this ongoing thing with her very tall, slender lawyer daughter, Liz, about the half-inch difference in their height. It gives them something to argue about in a relationship that is so palsy-walsy perfect that it's often hard to distinguish the parent from the child.

"Early in my life, I was more the grown-up and Mom was more the child," Liz says, alluding to the only real issue that existed between them. "Then when I was about twenty, she just decided to be the grown-up and for a while got to be much too controlling."

"The truth is," Irene says, "I tried very hard not to be controlling, because my mother was a very controlling person, and I didn't like the way I was brought up. Basically I had only three rules in the house. One: be polite. Two: never hurt yourself or anybody else. Three: the person who uses the last piece of toilet paper has to replace the roll. And no TV, except for PBS when appropriate."

"My mother was involved in a power struggle with her mother from the time I was an infant," Liz explains. "I remember we went to visit my grandmother in Michigan when I was about five. She was this old Polish woman with very strong ideas. I was wearing my hair shoulder length, like it is now, and tucking it behind my ears. She was afraid this was going to make my ears stick out the rest of my life and I would never get a husband. She kept saying I had to cut my hair, and my mother refused, mostly because she didn't want her mother to cut her daughter's hair. Personally I didn't care.

"About three in the morning, my grandmother came into my bedroom with a shears while I was asleep, picked up my head and cut off my hair. That was how she got her way. When I came to breakfast and had no hair, my mother went insane, and World War III broke out in Dearborn, Michigan, because she realized her mother always had to have the last word. That's why Mom tried so hard not to be controlling when I was growing up."

"I made lots of mistakes," Irene says openly. "I certainly had no parenting skills. My mother's parenting was all I knew and I didn't like it, yet I'd snap at the children with her words. You can read Dr. Spock to find out what the green goo is on the baby's diaper, but Dr. Spock cannot replace all the stuff you heard again and again and again from your own mother. I wish I had been more clever, and when I heard myself acting like my mother, I could have stopped and said: Now, wait a minute. My mother did that. Let me think about what *I* want to do here."

Today these lingering control issues have become something Irene and Liz can laugh about.

"Mom will call and remind me to do something, like 'Did you write that thank-you note?' "

"I try to think of creative ways to ask her so she doesn't know I'm asking," Irene says. "But it definitely is my control thing. And Liz will yell, 'You're doing it again. Stop it. Shut up. I can't stand it.' "

"What's great," Liz adds, "is that nothing hangs over us. The big storm comes and the air is always cleared. We say what we mean and we mean what we say. If we hurt each other's feelings, we apologize and go on."

"And I'm okay when Liz says no to me," Irene points out. "Like if I'm making chicken soup, I'll make double to give some to her because I know she's running around and doing her lawyer stuff and not thinking about supper."

"Mom's become her mother that way," Liz says warmly. "She feeds us all the time. Sometimes I'll say, 'No, thanks. You've fed us for the past week and we're going out for sushi.' "

"And that's cool with me," Irene explains. "But my mother would have sulked over that."

They've managed to strike that ideal balance between mother/daughter and friend.

"Liz gives me the best presents," Irene says.

"Likewise," Liz agrees.

"And I have to keep myself from calling her six or seven times a day," Irene goes on. "I'll see a fabulous scarf in a store or the dogs will do something I think she'd find funny."

"She even asked my husband if it's a pain for him that she calls all the time," Liz says. "He was very sweet. He said, 'No. I wish I could call my mother like that.' "

They often travel together and leave their partners at home. "We took the guys a couple of times, but it wasn't the same," Irene explains. "They don't get the quirkiness and funkiness of experiences like we do." Irene turns to Liz. "Remember that vibrator story?" Without another word they laugh hysterically.

They have an infinite store of wonderful shared memories. Good ones like the wedding dress Irene made for Liz. "Mom had made all my Halloween costumes and most of my clothes as a child and I thought it would be really nice to have her make my wedding dress." And painful ones: "When my parents divorced, that was the worst time. I was in college and Mom kind of lost it. She didn't ask for alimony and she had no money and no direction. She was living in Colorado and I was in New York and I was terrified because I didn't know where her next meal was coming from."

"Neither did I," Irene remembers. "I was so incredibly poor. What is so wonderful about Liz is whenever I've let her down, she has consistently forgiven me."

"C'mon, Mom," Liz says, "I never felt you let me down. You make everybody feel good. It's so great to go around town and have people say, 'I love your mother.' "

Suddenly they both become very serious. Irene breaks the silence. "I look at you, Liz, at your grace and your beauty and I think this is my joy. You seem so miraculous. If I were to create a daughter, any daughter in the world, it would be you. If I had all the parts and added some arms, legs, some soul, whatever I wanted, you are what I would come up with."

Elsa Malmud and her daughters, Anne and Susan Malmud

Somewhere around the time of her forty-second birthday and her twenty-first wedding anniversary, Elsa Malmud remembered that she'd forgotten to have children.

"I'd always planned on having kids," she says, "but I wasn't really ready until my forties. Other things kept getting in the way. First, it took me a long time to get my degrees. [She is a licensed clinical psychologist with a master's in school psychology and a doctorate in developmental psychology.] Then I really needed to have a career and make a contribution. I'd grown up without much of an identity. I went from being the daughter of very accomplished parents to somebody's wife, and I had such a need to be myself. Besides, it never occurred to me I would *not* get pregnant when I was ready. I was still menstruating. I'd never smoked or drank. And all the women in my family had babies."

Nevertheless, she made an appointment with a fertility specialist. But by the time he could see her, she'd already become pregnant without any intervention—which was rather remarkable considering that she and her husband hadn't used any birth control for years.

For the first five months of her pregnancy she didn't tell a soul because the skeptical doctor kept saying, "This could be the month you'll miscarry." When she did finally break the news to her mother, the reaction registered a big, fat zero on the enthusiasm scale. "She thought I was too old," Elsa explains. "She was worried about my age and my physical well-being."

Elsa, on the other hand, wasn't worried about anything. "I was just very, very happy, especially when I found out I was going to have a girl." Not until several months after her daughter's birth did Elsa face the reality of what it meant to postpone children. Tests showed her darling baby Susan was hearing-impaired and profoundly retarded.

"That's when I started to think about being old," Elsa says. "Had Susan been born when I was twenty-four, I would have taken care of her most of her life.

But being forty-four, I knew there'd come a time when she would be a young adult, and I'd be too old and have to put her in an institution. That realization was a great motivator. I couldn't do anything about the retarded part but, damn it, I'd see to it that she learned to talk, so if somebody abused her in that institution, she would be able to report it. Then and there, I decided she was going to be in the hearing world and not dependent on sign language."

On the advice of an audiologist, Elsa called a young friend and colleague who had a youngster the same age as Susan. "I have a retarded, deaf child who needs to be around other kids to learn to talk properly," she said rather pathetically. "Can I bring her to your house to play with your son."

The answer was "Of course."

"Every week, like a zombie, I took Susan there for a whole day," Elsa says. "This friend and my mother were the first to notice she wasn't the least bit retarded." While Susan lacked verbal skills at that point, she was quick to figure things out, suggesting that her developmental ability was perfectly normal. Elsa, the trained professional, had been too blinded by worry to see it. "You're not a psychologist with your own child," she explains. "You're only a mother."

Today, with the help of powerful hearing aids hidden under her unruly curls, Susan attends a regular school, where she ranks somewhere in the middle of her third-grade class. Listening to her clear speech, you'd have no idea she has a hearing problem. "She's just an extraordinary, wonderful child," her mother says. "People love her. She works like a dog to be like other kids. When everyone started music lessons, she wanted to play the piano. She can't hear most of her mistakes, but in the little workshops the teacher puts on, she performs right along with everybody else. She takes dancing lessons, too, and her friends help her when the teacher says put out your right leg and she sticks out her left arm because she can't hear."

Even if Susan hadn't overcome her handicap, Elsa immediately planned on having a second child. "This time I was very conscious of my age," she says, "and I didn't intend for her to be alone in the world." After six years of struggling with a fertility specialist, Elsa conceived Anne when she was fifty-one years old.

Is she sorry she waited so long? Not at all—although she has a few regrets: "I'm not going to be with the girls a lot of their life, especially Anne. When she is thirty, I'll be eighty-three—if I live that long. I doubt if I'll ever see grandchildren. And I won't be there to help my daughters with them. I couldn't live without my mother's help. She's turning eighty and is more with it than I will ever be. She is my best source of advice."

But Elsa is quick to dismiss those niggardly drawbacks and concentrate on her advantages. "I know myself," she says. "I've done a lot of the things I wanted. I've traveled, had a career and made sure my marriage would last before I had children. Besides, we're too tired to get a divorce. I didn't have to start exercising after the baby was born, because at this stage in my life it's okay to have a big stomach. And unlike some of my friends, I don't have to buy a dog and parakeet because my children have grown up and moved to California."

Moreover, Elsa has made the amazing discovery that babies in midlife take the place of Prozac.

"I believe middle age can be a very sad time," she says. "Friends and family get sick and die. People you trust betray you. You have to confront your mortality. Given enough time, I could obsess all day long about all the things I should've, would've, could've changed. Nobody has a corner on depression like I do.

"But then I come home and there are these two little children who laugh and smile, and everything is going well for them, and they just pull you into life. How can I sit and brood when I have diapers to change, formula to make, Susan needs help with homework and has a birthday party to go to? They don't let me sit around and drown. Before I know it I'm laughing and I'm running. By the time Anne leaves the house I'll be through my midlife crisis and settled into a cheery old lady."

Meanwhile, except for occasionally feeling out of sync with other women her age, Elsa is perfectly comfortable in her mothers' group with women ten to twenty years her junior. And she finds herself a good deal more relaxed than they are about child rearing.

"They want to make sure their kids are properly stimulated and eat the right health foods and wear clothes that are environmentally friendly and get to gymnastics to develop their muscles. I feel babies are stimulated enough crawling on the carpet. Anne will have to manage with formula instead of breast milk, and I'm so booked up that she'll never get to the gym. She'll just have to cope."

As for attempting to keep up with younger mothers, Elsa doesn't even try. "Every mother has things she can give her kid and things she can't. I don't have to Rollerblade for Susan to learn how—and I wouldn't have done that even if I were twenty years younger, because I'm a klutz. The last time I went roller-skating I broke my arm. I'm not good at art, but not because I'm fifty-three. I've never been good at art. I'm not all that fun a person and I'm not hip. I wasn't hip at twenty. But Susan and I read together and go places and talk. I attend all the school events, and I'm a room mother."

Sometimes that role takes a bit of explaining, because the other children tend to think she's the room *grand*mother.

"When we go into a new situation I let the kids know right away that I'm Susan's mother. At day camp one visiting day a little kid asked me if I was Susan's grandma, because I had gray hair and wrinkles. I said, 'No. I look old, but I'm her mom.' And she said, 'Oh, I understand that. My dad is sixty-five.'"

Only once was Elsa crushed by a reference to her age. It was after she'd become pregnant with Anne when a thoughtless relative asked her how she could possibly consider having another child when she was already such an embarrassment to Susan.

"I almost never cry," Elsa says, "but I sat up all night weeping until Susan woke up and I offered to dye my hair black."

Susan, a delightfully open and precocious nine-year-old, remembers that discussion of her mother's age and appearance with perfect clarity—and she dismisses it as something hardly worth talking about.

"If kids don't know me, they might think my mom's a grandma, but I don't feel embarrassed about it," she says breezily. "I never think at all about Mom being older. I think how surprising it is that she can be doing so much more stuff than other moms.

"Anyway, I remember somebody told her she should dye her hair because I was really ashamed it was gray. We talked about it and I said, 'No. I like you better with gray hair than any other color 'cause that's what's natural for you. It doesn't bother me one bit.' Really it doesn't. My friends don't care what my mom looks like. They only care that she isn't mean."

Elsa beams at having passed the critical test. "I am who I am," she says with the confidence born of maturity. "Hopefully I'll be a good enough mother so that Susan and Anne will grow up into happy, nice, useful people. Frankly, given all my inadequacies, if they only complain that I'm rickety and old, I'll die happy."

Dolly Earl and Barbara Nelson and their daughter, Lea Jayne Ferrer

Barbara Nelson sits on a cracked vinyl chair in the Spokane airport waiting lounge, nervously picking specks of lint from her neatly pressed simple skirt and blouse. Her hair is freshly done; her heart is pounding like a train engine. In fifteen minutes the daughter she gave up for adoption so long ago will step off the plane and into the loving embrace she has been saving for her these twenty-seven anguished years.

BARBARA'S STORY

"I didn't have an easy time growing up. I never really knew my own mother. She died when I was three and my sister and I were separated and raised by different members of the family. When I was twenty-one, I fell in love with a guy and followed him to Las Vegas. Soon I learned I was pregnant and I was too scared and ashamed to tell anybody. He wanted me to have an abortion, and when I refused, he left me. He didn't want the responsibility. But he came back and we got married and for a little while we were happy. He still didn't want the baby, though, and I was so afraid of losing him. I had to make a choice. Finally I agreed we should give up the child for adoption.

"I called my daughter Rosa, little rose. I rubbed her little hands and feet and thought: What am I doing giving this up? I cried and cried and they had to give me something to sleep that night. In the morning I signed the papers. It feels so funny when you come home without a baby. It's like it died. That's what my husband wrote and told my sister. That I'd had a premature baby that was born dead. She didn't know the truth until way later. I just never could get over the hurt. I had given up something so precious and I wished I'd never done it."

Barbara's marriage went from bad to worse. She had a second daughter, Liza, in the same hospital where Rosa had been born. This time she took her baby home. Finally, after four years of her husband's carousing and womanizing, she left and worked as a chambermaid to support herself and her child. Eventually she remarried, had another daughter and two sons and moved to Minnesota, where she works nights in a factory to help make ends meet.

"But I never forgot about Rosa. Every year on her birthday I wondered: How is she doing? Is she being raised by a good family? I worried about everything. The hurt was always there. And I always told Liza that someday we'd find her big sister. So when Rosa turned nineteen, the legal age when you can start to search, I contacted the agency back in Nevada and notified them that I wanted to find my daughter.

"Ten years went by. I was starting to lose hope, thinking I had to teach myself to let go and get on with my life. And then six weeks ago, I got a call from the agency and the lady said, 'Well, I found your daughter. Do you want to speak to her?' I was crying and excited and crying and so happy. I gave my husband the phone because I didn't think I would get the number right. Then I thought: I better make that call fast before I lose courage. I was so scared and nervous about how she was going to accept me. You can't imagine what I felt when I heard her voice for the first time. 'I don't know if you know me,' I said. 'I'm Barbara Nelson. I'm your mother.' And I told her that I've always loved her.

"What am I hoping for? Well, I don't want to take the role of her adopted mother. That much I respect. I can see she raised her good and I appreciate that. I don't care what she calls me. I just want to be her mom and for us to be good friends because she's my daughter."

Dolly Earl fastens her seat belt and reassuringly pats the arm of her adopted daughter, Lea, as the plane enters its descent into Spokane. She thinks about the woman waiting on the ground who gave her the gift of this wonderful child. For twenty-seven years Dolly has wanted to say thank you, and soon she will have that chance.

DOLLY'S STORY:

"My husband and I always wanted a big family, but we had a genetic problem with Rh disease. Our second son had to have a transfusion and it was pretty devastating to go through. Then I had a third baby and she lived only one day. You feel close to the Lord when you go through something hard like this and we thought we would not be able to have any more children, so right away we decided to adopt. Then six months later, boom, we were given Lea. For six months I had cried for the daughter I'd lost, and when I got Lea, I didn't cry anymore.

"To our surprise, I went on to have two more daughters. But I can tell you there is no difference. I have said a thousand times that I have an adopted daughter, but I forget which one. Still, there is a special bond with Lea because she came at a time when I needed her so desperately.

"My boys are wonderful, too. But every woman wants a daughter to share feelings with, and that's what Lea and I have done. She says we're not best friends. That I'm always going to be her mother and she wants to keep me there. But we *are* best friends. We do things together all the time.

"I always talked to Lea about being adopted and how I held her mother in reverence and appreciated that she gave birth to a child for us. We talked for years about her finding her mother. I wanted her to do it. She needed it. Everyone needs roots.

"I never felt threatened. Lea loves me and I love her and we're fine. We're both mature women. I believe we can love a lot of people. If you love a lot, love expands and grows. What we're doing is tucking in a few more people. I think Barbara and I will be friends. We'll feel like kin. I can't wait to meet her."

Lea stares into her compact mirror, checking her flawless makeup with the trained eye she's developed as a beauty consultant for Chanel cosmetics. She wants to look perfect for this mother she's never met, yet underneath her cool facade her stomach is doing flip-flops. Did she make the right decision to search for her birth mother? What will Barbara expect of her? What will she be like? Lea dabs the black smudge in the corner of her eye. Tears and mascara just don't mix.

LEA'S STORY:

"I've always been proud and happy I was adopted. I remember being told over and over that I was specially chosen. But when people meet our family it's obvious that I look different. It's always been important to me to know where I'm from. Where did I get this pale skin, these eyes, these hands?

"It never occurred to me to look for my father. When I think of a mother I think about nurturing and caring, and I always thought of him as probably the way he is. But it took me forever to mail the application because part of me was afraid.

"When the agency called to say they'd found my mother, I remember I started shaking and bawling. I was totally at a loss for words. And I am never at a loss for words! Then my phone rang and it was *her!* I told her, 'I always knew you existed. I've always loved the image of you in my mind and in my heart.' Right away she said, 'I want to tell you why I did it.' It didn't matter to me, but it was important to her.

"I've always thought my mother must have had great compassion. I believe that when you give up a baby for adoption, it shows you have respect for yourself and for the baby you're carrying. You're not selfish. Selfish is abortion. Selfish is having a kid and living a horrible lifestyle. I know these feelings aren't in sync with most adopted kids, but this is how my parents raised me.

"I'm not sure how Barbara will fit into my life now. I don't need another mother. I bonded with Dolly as a baby and that's a bond that can't be broken. She has filled the space as my mother all these years. She's been with me in good times, hard times, bad times, great times. No, I'm not looking for a replacement in a mother. I think Barbara will be more like a very close aunt."

The plane touched down at 10:45. They all literally fell into each other's arms, crying and laughing and hugging . . . and praying that this would be the beginning of a brand-new extended family. Little by little they would fill in the gaps of past history and create a future of shared memories.

In finding her mother, Lea might finally be able to open herself to love freely. "There is a natural fear you have when you've been put up for adoption that keeps you from getting super close to anyone," she says. "If your own mother, your flesh and blood, could give you up, why would anybody else who met me later down the road want to stick around? I think meeting my mother and feeling all this love from her will help me let go of my fear of being hurt."

And in finding her daughter, Barbara has found peace. "I always worried about Rosa. I mean Lea. I always wondered if she was okay. Now I know she's fine and that puts my heart at rest."

Lindy Boggs and her daughter, Cokie Roberts

Several years ago ABC television reporter Cokie Roberts found herself in a bank refinancing her mortgage, which just happened to be for the suburban Washington home where she'd grown up. (She and her husband loved it so much they bought it from her mother.) The clerk handed Cokie a form to sign, muttering, "This is nothing important. Just a boilerplate saying we haven't discriminated against you because of sex, race, marital status, etc."

Cokie stared at him indignantly. "Nothing!" she hissed. "This is not *nothing*. My mother wrote that law!"

She turns to the delicate, eighty-year-old former congresswoman perched on a silk sofa beside her, and they both giggle. The sound of their laughter is identical. "When Mom was in the House of Representatives and I was covering Congress," Cokie says, "there's a place in the back of the lobby that's reserved just for House members and the press. I would be there doing an interview and I'd laugh, and somebody would turn around and say, 'Oh, excuse me. I thought Mrs. Boggs was here.' We sounded so much alike."

"That was a great time for us," Lindy remembers. "We could catch up with each other without having to make an appointment. We had a rule. I gave Cokie no leaks and she gave me no coverage."

Lindy speaks in the lilting drawl of a Louisiana belle and she lives according to the code of manners drummed into well-bred Southern women of her age and class. "Pleasing others is something that's pleasing to me," she says simply. "It's how I grew up."

Christened Marie Corinne Morrison Claiborne, she was nicknamed Lindy by a baby nurse who thought she looked just like her father, Rolande. In the family tradition of lengthy names, she called her third-born child Mary Martha Corinne Morrison Claiborne Boggs. She was dubbed Cokie by her older brother, who couldn't pronounce Corinne, and it stuck.

"One of the main things I learned from watching my mother operate as a

Southern woman is that gentility and grace are the most effective tools," Cokie says, pulling a yellow thread through the scrim of a needlepoint pillow. "If your goal is to get something done, do it as softly as possible. Don't blow your own horn and don't take a lot of credit.

"The other thing was not to lay guilt on your children. My mother was always the great guilt eraser rather than the guilt inculcator. I think most women of my age have difficult relationships with their mothers because they're doing things their mothers never had the opportunity to do—which makes them jealous—or they're *not* doing what their mothers did—which is staying home and raising their children properly. My mother is completely the opposite. She has a very fulfilled life. She approves of what I do and knows how a woman can balance her career, her family and her contributions to the community."

Despite having had enormously successful careers, this mother and daughter both place a very high priority on their roles as mothers and keepers of the hearth.

"I absolutely want to be the kind of mother my mother was," Cokie says. "My daughter is also my buddy and I was very unhappy when she went to college. Not only was I losing my baby who was now all grown up, but I had to redefine myself— because my first definition of me had been as a mother.

"It would be unthinkable," she continues, "not to run my home like my mother did, not to make it a special place where people feel comfortable and welcome or not to do all the traditional children things or holiday parties. Every year I do Hanukkah *and* Christmas, Passover *and* Easter for about forty-five people. [She is Catholic; her husband is Jewish.] It's not that my mother laid some kind of trip on me about this. It's that I grew up surrounded by friends and relatives and it's what I loved."

Lindy leans forward. "Well, why can't women do it all?" she asks boldly. "What about your great-great-grandmother who managed to cross the ocean? I was raised by six of the most

remarkable, accomplished women whose parents were suffragettes and they expected a great deal from me."

But they didn't expect Lindy to take her husband's place in Congress. Hale Boggs died in 1973 when his plane disappeared over Alaska; it was never found. Nor was she expected to serve eight terms (she retired in 1990) or to establish a memorable record as a respected voice in the Democratic Party and a leader in legislation for women's economic rights. "Mother's evolving identification with women's issues was interesting," Cokie notes. "Nothing creates a feminist faster than being widowed or divorced."

Although Lindy never planned on being anything more than an involved political wife, Cokie wasn't surprised when her mother ran for her father's vacated seat—and won. "It was natural," she says. "Certain families have certain talents. Some people know how to do math; some art. We do politics."

Despite raising her three children in a political fishbowl and jockeying their chaotic lives between Washington and their home base in New Orleans, Lindy managed to leave the impression she was a typical full-time mom.

"My memory of my childhood," Cokie says, "was of my mother being around all the time—and she really wasn't. Intellectually I knew that a lot of the time she and Dad were away or out to dinner, but she was so emotionally available that we had the sense of being this wonderful happy family. My mother made our household safe, loving, caring and *fun*. She even found time to sew our clothes."

Lindy smiles modestly. "I used to say I slept fast."

"Maybe one of the reasons I never went through a rebellious period was that my life was so pleasant," Cokie goes on. "Mother wasn't strict, but she had expectations that you behaved in a certain way. If you didn't she was disappointed, which was horrible, so you didn't do anything to encourage that."

Lindy's view of discipline centered on the punishment chair, a little upholstered piece of furniture that sits today in her classically elegant, photo-filled Washington apartment. Cokie was required to sit in the chair when she misbehaved to think about what she'd done wrong.

"I have memories," she says, "of being there for long periods of time."

As might be expected, politics dominated the family's dinner-table talk, and it was often heated, since Hale Boggs was that rare bird in the civil rights era: a Southern liberal. The children actively participated in his campaigns and Lindy was a great believer in having them skip school if there were more important lessons elsewhere.

"I completely missed learning long division," Cokie says, "because the day it was taught we were taken to hear Daddy appear before a state committee to answer charges about being a Communist. We all went up to Baton Rouge, and I remember Earl Long kept pulling out his medicine, which was a bottle filled with liquor. I thought it was a scream."

This priceless ringside seat in the world of politics proved to be perfect grooming for Cokie's work covering the Washington scene, first on radio for NPR and later with ABC television. "The only time my mother is critical of me," Cokie says, "is when she thinks I ask tough questions on television. But she has never done what most people's mothers do, which is complain about my hair or how I look."

"The great thing about Cokie is the substance of what she's doing and saying and thinking," Lindy breaks in. "If she also happens to look beautiful, that's wonderful. I've had people say, 'I wouldn't miss Cokie on Sunday morning. She had on this beautiful jacket and she looked so pretty.' And I'd say, 'Gosh, I missed the show. What were they *talking* about?' 'I don't remember, darling, but you should have *seen* her!'"

Cokie's mouth slides into her characteristic bemused grin and she shakes her head. "You can say the smartest, dumbest, meanest or fanciest thing on TV and people will still notice your hair."

In 1990 Cokie assumed a new role in her mother's life—she became an only daughter when her sister Barbara, the mayor of Princeton, New Jersey, died from cancer. "I came to understand early in Barbara's illness," Cokie says, "that my old age would not be what I had expected. But what I didn't know until she died, and what came as a horrible shock, was that my memory would also be gone, because I no longer had my older sister to check things with."

"Cokie takes the responsibility of worrying about me very seriously," Lindy says.

"It's not hard," Cokie answers. "I love being with Mother. I feel blessed to have her so vibrant and wonderful at this point in her life. But I do worry that she's a bit old and half the time I don't know where she is. She's hard to find. Since I'm the only daughter, I do want to know she's okay. I would take her to live with me, but getting her there would be an interesting feat. Mother likes being on her own."

"Well," Lindy says in her defense, "I was raised to be self-sufficient and develop my initiative."

And clearly that is how she raised her children.

Are you like your mother, Cokie?

"We are both gregarious, hospitable people," she answers. "And the things that are good about me are from my mother."

That thought seems to unravel her. She puts down her needlepoint to wipe her eyes. "But I'm not as good as my mother. I love her very much."

Lindy strokes her daughter's hand. "Well, you better," she says tenderly. "You better."

Ann Clark, her daughter, Catherine Clark Schwartz, and granddaughters Rebecca and Hannah

A daughter can never really know her mother until she becomes a mother herself and begins to rethink and relive her mother's life.

"Before I had children," Kate says, "I could see things only from my own perspective and how they affected *me*—and I projected that onto Mummy. Now that I'm a mother, that's changed and I am able to see things much more from my mother's point of view."

Fortunately, Kate did not need the experience of motherhood to heal any wounds carried over from her childhood. "In most ways I was a model daughter," she says. "Miss Sensible. Very capable. My idea of rebellion was to dye my hair peroxide blond and experiment with my clothes. So except for my teenage years when I got a little rebellious, Mummy and I always had a good relationship. Maybe not the blunt honesty of some people, but we were very close. I have seven brothers, and I think that colored things somewhat."

The second of nine children—and the feistiest of the lot—Kate was the only daughter for fifteen years until her baby sister was born. At eighteen she left her hometown of Armagh, the ecclesiastical capital of Ireland, to go off to college in Scotland, where she got her degree as a primary-school teacher. Today she lives in Amsterdam and London, the only one of her siblings who has strayed far from the nest. She remembers her childhood as quite happy, despite her role as "mini-mom."

"I definitely relied on Kate to be a mother's helper," Ann confesses. "It's a horrible thing to say but I expected my daughters to see things in a different perspective and be more independent and intelligent than my sons. I think daughters have an intuition about things, and sons, in general, need to be taught. Boys take it for granted that they will be looked after and things will be done for them. Girls don't."

"Mummy was always more protective of the boys," Kate says. "I remember once when I was, maybe, twenty-one and my brother Simon was seventeen. She was cleaning the fruit bowl and there was one apple left. She said, 'Who would like it?' and we both answered, 'I would.' Instead of dividing the apple in two, Mummy gave the whole apple to my brother."

Ann tries to explain. "If there was only one apple and I had wanted it and so did somebody else, I would have naturally given it to the other person. I immediately thought: Kate is like me, so she'd give it over. That's why I didn't even ask her if she minded."

Kate responds, "My mother has always assumed that I was like her and I resented her for being so selfless. I believe women are people who are equal to men, and I wanted her to think of herself more. But she lived for her children and didn't require anything in return. You could have been a little bitch and she still would have come up with the same love.

"Now that I have children, I understand that's what a mother's love is. I do the same things with my girls that my mother did with me, something I could never understand until I became a mother myself. While I always respected my mother, because she is very, very strong in a quiet way, now I respect her even more. I find it terribly difficult to give my two girls all the attention they need, and my mother managed to treat nine of us as individuals."

Having daughters of her own has deepened Kate's feelings for her mother on many levels. "Before I had children, I wanted to have two boys," Kate says intently. "I had this romantic idea that I would be a young, glamorous woman with two teenage sons who were going to look after me. But since my girls were born, I realized I don't need a son. There is a much different relationship between a mother and daughter, an unspoken understanding that you can't have with a boy.

"I am most thankful to my mother that she gave me free rein to become whoever I was. She never, ever forced her views on me or tried to make me into what she wanted me to be. Even when she didn't like my breast-feeding, she wasn't what I'd call critical."

"You were very tired," Ann says, "and you had trouble with your breasts and I thought: Oh, why bother? I didn't see why you had to go through that pain."

"She couldn't see me suffering," Kate says knowingly. "I think this is something a lot of daughters come up against. Their mothers continue to treat them as their daughters and not as the mother of the baby."

"Well," Ann says, speaking for every mother, "you will always be first and foremost my daughter, and second, the mother of your children. I had you first and you are still mine."

Gwen Sherman and
her daughter, Amber Sherman

The short, happy life of Amber Sherman began at 7:47 A.M. on July 16, 1976. She weighed 7 pounds 5 ounces at birth and was 21 inches long. By age five she'd grown to 36 pounds and 45 inches. At 19 she weighed 125 and had reached the height of 5 feet 7 inches. The newspaper headlines on the day she was born trumpeted riots in South Africa, fighting in Beirut and the U.S. bicentennial celebration. Her twenty-year-old mother, Gwen, was thrilled to have a baby girl, especially one as perfect as Amber with her white-gold hair, big, round blue-gray eyes and precious smile. By age two Amber was potty-trained and speaking in sentences. One of her first was "I lob you." Amber's only serious childhood illnesses were tonsillitis and impetigo. She learned to ride a bike at age six, play the guitar at age twelve and drive a car at age sixteen. Her earliest hobby was collecting baseball cards; her ambition, to be a cowgirl. By high school she'd changed her mind and decided to become a chef.

Amber's history is laid out in her photo albums. A smiling second grader with no front teeth; a seventh grader with braces. Little Amber making peepee in a sand bucket at Rehoboth Beach. Amber in her first ballet costume; Amber dressed as a cat for Halloween; Amber dancing in a Mexican restaurant where the MC asked for someone to come onstage and she volunteered. Amber a tan, slender teenager on the deck of a cruise ship. Amber riding a camel on a vacation somewhere. Amber jumping into the swimming pool at a hotel in the Caribbean. Amber posing, a tad awkwardly, in her first formal gown. Amber and a foreign exchange student, her first and only love. Amber standing stiffy in her crisp white chef's jacket by an elaborate cake she'd decorated. Amber delivering the valedictory address at her graduation in sunglasses because "her future was so bright she had to wear shades."

Amber Sherman was meticulous—she won the all-star award for neatness in kindergarten. She was talented—she played a mean guitar and excelled at computers. And she was very smart. Her twelfth-grade report card lists chemistry

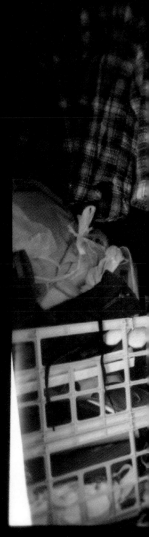

93, English 93, economics 95, Spanish 94, computer design 97, times tardy 0, times absent 3. She was on the honor roll continuously from seventh grade and a member of the National Honor Society who graduated with a $500 scholarship from the Baltimore Trust Company and the State Superintendent's Scholar Award.

Amber Sherman was also a decent and well-loved human being. When a high school classmate—a casual friend—couldn't redeem a savings bond in time to raise the spending money necessary for their class trip, Amber dipped into her $600 savings account and loaned the girl $300, despite her mother's admonition that she'd never get it back. She did—but it wouldn't have mattered to her either way.

Amber loved doing nice things for people. That's why she'd agreed to go in to work early on that cool September morning. One of the bakery's customers needed extra pastries for her wedding reception and the regular baker was too busy to make them. Amber, always willing to go the extra mile, offered to come in and do the baking herself. In less than a month she'd be leaving her summer job at the bake shop to move into her first apartment and start her second year at the Culinary Institute. At 5:30 on Saturday, September 16, 1995, as the rosy light of dawn bathed the highway, Amber slid behind the wheel of her car. She hadn't gone very far when a drunk, some guy who'd been up all night partying, rammed into her. He walked away with a cut on his ear. Amber was killed instantly.

She was nineteen years old, reduced to nothing but a memory.

· · ·

Gwen got the call at 9 A.M. as she was getting into the shower. The policeman said, "Your daughter's been involved in an accident and we want to come over to talk to you."

"Is she hurt?" Gwen cried, already starting to feel sick. "Is she in the hospital? Has she been killed?"

"Well, it's better if we come and talk to you," the young cop replied.

And Gwen knew right away. It's the nightmare every mother has. She just knew. Policemen don't make those calls unless it's the worst news. She sank down on the floor, too numb to cry. A void exploded in her life that nothing would ever fill.

"When the police told me Amber was dead, the first thing I thought of is that nobody will remember her in ten years. I'm so afraid she'll disappear. Nobody will remember my responsible, intelligent, beautiful daughter. She left this huge hole in me. An emptiness I can't describe.

"This jacket I'm wearing belonged to her. Amber and I always wore each other's clothes. She was my adviser on hair and clothes. We'd go shopping and she'd say, 'If you want to look like an old person, go ahead and buy that.' When she went away to school she wrote me a card saying, 'How will we divide our clothes now?'

"I was never one to reminisce, but I've become very sentimental. This ring is hers. I put it on right after she died. It was the diamond from the engagement ring her father gave me, and after our divorce I had it reset for her as a sixteenth birthday gift. I think I'll wear it forever.

"I still can't bear to change anything in her room. Sometimes I'll just go into her closet and smell her clothes. I laid out some of her things on her bed—her chef's cap, her white jacket and the little black box with her knives in it. I used to sleep in her bed when she first went away to school because I wanted to feel close to her. But I can't do that anymore.

"We were more like best friends than mother and daughter. We did all kinds of things together. Skiing. Horseback riding. Deep-sea diving. Going out to dinner. How can I replace that? What can I do with this sadness? I just go on. I have to go on. But I miss everything about her. I've been robbed of her future. And mine, too, in a way. I won't be able to watch her grow and become independent and move into her career. Get married and have children. She was an only child, so there won't be any grandchildren for me.

"I was thinking, too, how I've become a lot closer to my mother as I've gotten older, and I realize that I won't be able to have that deepening relationship with Amber. When I'm old in the nursing home, I won't have anybody to call."

Gwen's sobs overcome her. "Forgive me," she says after a few minutes. "I still can't talk about Amber without crying.

"It just feels like somebody ripped my heart out. The oddest little things come out of nowhere and remind me of her. I was watching a movie about Alcatraz the other night and I wanted to call her and ask her if she'd been there on her high school trip to San Francisco. This winter when it started to snow, I instinctively reached for the phone to call her at school in New York to see if it was snowing there yet. I'm torn between wanting to run away and have nothing remind me of her—and never leaving, because everything reminds me of her.

"I was at a dinner not long ago and a woman asked me if I had any children. I didn't know how to answer her, but I said, 'Yes, I do.' One of the worst things is that I don't understand what my role is now. Not a day goes by that I don't think of Amber. In my heart, in that way, I'll be Amber's mother forever. But am I still a mother if I don't have my daughter?"

Sharon Cantrell and her daughters, Christi Driver, Lori Sommerfeld and Betsy McLaughlin

What happens to a mother when her dreams for her daughters turn out to be nothing at all like the dreams they have for themselves?

"I wanted my girls to have choices," Sharon Cantrell says. But not necessarily the choices they made.

Lori, her eldest daughter, tells how the girls saw it. "We all knew what Mom wanted for us. She didn't want us to get pregnant before we were married, because she did at nineteen and she and Dad had no education and no money and it was a struggle. Since she didn't graduate from college before her marriage, her dream was that we'd all get our degrees. We would all live in the same area. We would come to her house on Sunday for dinner and go to her Protestant church, where we'd all sit together with our children in the designated pew. And I kinda blew it. I married a Catholic and converted and I didn't finish college and become a teacher. My number one dream in life was just to become a mom."

And because Lori is an exemplary mother to her three children and displays the most organized, Tupperware-filled cabinets in her entire neighborhood, Sharon managed to let go of her dreams for daughter number one without too much of a struggle. *So they wouldn't go to church together. So what!* There were more pressing problems with Betsy, who was busy putting her own dents in her mother's Norman Rockwell-perfect-American-family portrait.

In Betsy's sophomore year of high school she brought her new boyfriend, Al, home to meet her folks. Al was perfectly nice—but he was black.

"I never thought there was any problem," Betsy says.

Sharon starts to laugh. "Betsy, where were you living? Remember, I was raised where appearances are everything. I had all these values about respecting differences, but when you came home with Al the first time, I said to myself: Hey, wait a minute. I wanted you to treat people equally—but I didn't mean in my home. We liked Al, but we thought your romance would pass and he would go away. When he didn't, I had to really struggle with those issues. It was a process of going from worrying what people thought to caring about Betsy."

Supporting Betsy became increasingly difficult and her black boyfriend was the least of it. "From age fifteen to twenty, Betsy was hell to raise," Sharon remembers. "We lived under the same roof yet barely spoke. She bounced off the edges of the rules."

Betsy careened through a semester of college, got pregnant, had an abortion and quit when her grade point average fell to 1.5. Then she met and married another man, also black, and pulled her life back onto a very traditional track which led to three cocoa-colored children whom their doting grandmother calls "her rainbow coalition."

So her darling grandchildren are of mixed race and their mother never did finish college. So what!

"Look at Betsy now," Sharon says with genuine pride. "She is just the neatest mother and the most wonderful woman. A lot of people think if they have rebellious teens there is no hope. But she turned out fine."

"Mom helped me be the person I am without crushing my spirit," Betsy says, quietly nursing her weeks-old infant.

That left Christi to fulfill her mother's hopes. She did, in fact, finish college. But by her thirtieth birthday she was divorced with a child—and ready to declare herself a lesbian.

"I wanted so badly to be successful in a traditional way," Christi says. "But I finally got so tired of hiding. No matter what, I was Mom's daughter and we had the common bond of that twenty-five percent of me. But I had to hide the other seventy-five percent of what I was. Because of that I was withdrawing from the family and I missed them. I needed their support."

Christi came out to her mother the day before Halloween. She'd let her mom deal with her dad later.

"I'd practiced all day long," Christi remembers. "Then I asked Mom to please come over that night. I was on the couch and she was on the love seat. 'What's wrong?' she asked me. 'Are you pregnant?' I said, 'No. But if I tell you this, I hope you can still care about me. I need you to know I'm gay.' And she started sobbing. Not because she was upset, she told me, but because she felt so sad that I had to carry this secret all by myself for so long. And I had this incredible sense of relief. Of feeling whole again and accepted and loved and safe.

"The next day at work, Mom sent me flowers with a card that said, 'I'm proud of you for standing up for what you believe. Thank you for trusting me. We love you unconditionally. Mom.' And our relationship has been even closer since—even though I knew I'd blown the dream."

Goodbye, Norman Rockwell. Hello, reality.

Sharon, who is now a social worker, has come not only to appreciate her daughters' lifestyles but to depend on them as people. "We've evolved into having this wonderful adult friendship," she says. "When I want the courage to do something, I will go to Betsy, because she is all the things I wanted to be and didn't have the guts to try. When I want nurturing, I go to Lori. And when I want an adult-to-adult, feminist, positive something, I go to Christi. I am so proud of my daughters and who they've become."

If it all looks too easy, Sharon is quick to point out the tears and pain it's taken to reach her place of acceptance. Yet she feels her world has expanded far beyond anything she could have imagined had her daughters followed her program. "Sometimes you plan a vacation to Italy and you wake up in Holland instead," she says. "It's not where you wanted to go, but it's a beautiful place just the same. I think when you have dreams for your children and they don't play out the way you dreamed, there is certainly a grieving process. But it's not a bad thing, because you can learn from it that everyone has a right to their own life. I've actually been lucky. I have had a wonderful journey."

Kate Shupe and her daughters, Joan, Nettie, Helen, Mary Lee, Lula Kate, Jane, Sally, Edith and Maria

As faithfully as the earth revolves around the sun, the Shupe family revolves around Mama Kate. At ninety-six, her back is as straight as a cutting board, her mind as sharp as her kitchen knives and her hands still strong enough to plant and tend her sprawling vegetable garden. But she would tell you that her "best of show" grew from the seeds nurtured within her own body.

Kate Goodman Shupe—"Mama" to some and "Granny" to others—was born in the very last year of the nineteenth century and was married during World War I to a man who worked all his life as a guard at a Virginia state hospital. On her wedding night she modestly undressed under the covers and in her fifty-eight years of marriage her husband never saw her naked.

She paid the doctor twenty dollars each time he delivered one of her thirteen children at home in her own bed until, at forty-two, she quit because her body said enough and stopped producing eggs. Mama Kate raised her brood during the Depression, fed them with food she farmed and cooked herself and often dressed them in clothes she sewed from feed bags. Every one of them finished high school; some graduated from college. When Kate was fifty-four she put aside her housework and took a job in a hospital until her retirement at sixty-two. Since then, she has visited all but six of the United States, most recently camping in a tent with one of her daughters. She was eighty when she finally traded in her wringer-washer for an automatic model. She still vacuums every day, makes quilts and aprons and faithfully sends birthday cards with a dollar inside to each of her twenty-four grandchildren and thirty great-grandchildren. She has survived her twelve brothers and sisters, her husband, who died of heart disease in 1976, two

daughters and one infant son, eighteen American Presidents and the loss of a cancerous kidney at age ninety. Seven of her nine daughters live within fifteen minutes of her Virginia home and every single Saturday night of the year, twenty or thirty of the clan gather together with Mama for a covered-dish supper.

Mama Kate's formula for living is as simple as her fried apple pie recipe: "I lived a straight life. I never used bad language—that's a sin. Never smoked. Never drank. Worked real hard. I never think about being tired and I never complain. God has given me good health. The girls ask me all the time, 'Mommy, are you stressed?' I say, 'Tell me how you feel when you're stressed and I'll know whether I am or not.' "

Her formula for mothering is equally uncomplicated: "I stayed right in the house with my children every day they were growing up. Always tried to treat all my girls the same. If I give one of them something, I try to give all of them something. I believe in equals. And I always told them to be nice. I said, 'If you lay down with dogs you get up with fleas.' They knew what I meant. When they were young, I said, 'When you're going with a boy, be nice and keep yourself clean. If a boy says anything to you out-of-the-way, pick up whatever you come across and knock him in the head with it.' "

Her daughters, all grown with children and grandchildren of their own, still lean on their mother as the foundation of their family. Joan explains: "I don't think any of us could be there for our two or three children the way Mama has been there looking after all twelve of us. No matter how busy she was, in the midst of baking bread or rolls, we'd come flying in and she would always take the time to listen and tend to us. She never had an automatic yes or no answer."

Mama Kate nods and smiles impishly. "The Bible says if you spare the rod, you spoil the child. Their daddy didn't spare the rod, so I had to spoil the children. They'd run to me for protection, crying and such. I'd talk to them and quiet their fussing. See, I was

raised to listen to my parents and obey what they told me and my girls listened pretty good to me." In a chorus they chime in, "We still do!"

God willing, Kate Shupe will celebrate her hundredth birthday the year before the millennium. In person or in spirit, how will her daughters remember Mama?

Sally: "She's very wise. If anyone in the family does something she thinks isn't quite right, she has a little chat with them, explaining what she doesn't approve of—and why she doesn't expect it to happen again. I don't think Mama ever made us feel bad about ourselves, and I'm sure there were times when I deserved it. She just instilled this feeling of security."

Edith: "She's loving. She just has this loving presence. And I'll always remember her cooking."

Maria: "I think of Mama as a lady. A staunch, upright, early American lady. She always taught us to be kind to our fellow man and considerate of our neighbors. When I lost my husband I was so distraught I lost my powers of reasoning. At four o'clock in the morning I called my sister and said I don't know what to do, and she said, 'Put on your housecoat and come over here.' Next morning I got a call from Mama. 'Girl, you can't do that. You've got to get yourself in order.' She taught us to be independent, responsible, strong women."

Nettie: "She's very comforting. During all my sickness, she keeps telling me, 'You go on now. Get up, don't worry, you're gonna be all right. You look good; you're coming along.' And that does make me feel better. It helps."

This memory triggers a similar one in Joan. "Mama's strength and comfort helps us overcome most anything. Several years ago I had major surgery and was getting ready to go talk with St. Peter. There's Mama standing over me when I'm throwing up tray after tray of blood, saying, 'Young'un, you have to do better. You have to fight this.' If you're lying there dying and you've got an eighty-five-year-old woman telling you this, you're gonna try and get up."

Helen: "She's very well-read. She watches the news, keeps up with what's going on in the world. She's interested in everything and everybody. And she's appreciative. Nothing you give her is too small that she doesn't appreciate it."

Mary Lee: "She's very kind. When my husband passed away, she came to me the first night and crawled in my bed and said, 'I'm going to sleep with you because it's important that I do this.' That was so very comforting. And when Papa died, we were so upset and Mama was the strong one. I will always remember her encouragement. She wanted us to get a good education so we could get good jobs, go out in the world and manage our lives. She gave us all self-esteem."

Lula Kate: "Mama is such a wonderful traveler. We never have to feel at all inhibited when she's with us, worrying there's something she might not like. She was always in our corner, making us feel secure and wanted. She taught us to accept responsibility and be independent and communicated to us by example, not by pressure. And she had such patience. When I

think of her having all those babies, taking care of us, cooking, doing laundry on a washboard, ironing with irons heated on the stove, milking cows, gardening, canning, feeding the chickens, helping Papa saw wood—how she managed is beyond my imagination."

Joan: "We were poor in money but we were not poor in spirit or material things. We had plenty of food, clothing and warmth. We made our own toys, sat around nights and sang. Colored eggs at Easter. Wonderful Christmas days. Life with Mama is never boring. She is just fascinating."

Jane: "We put her on a pedestal because she deserves it."

On the Saturday nights that the Shupe family gets together, it is not uncommon for Mama Kate to sit at the organ in her living room surrounded by her beaming daughters while she powerfully pumps out hymn after hymn. When they sing "Amazing Grace," all eyes focus on the erect woman at the keyboard. Amazing she surely is. Amazing Kate.